SENCO
at a glance

Also available from Continuum

- *At a Glance 2nd Edition: A Practical Guide to Children's Special Needs*, Viv East and Linda Evans
- *Surviving and Succeeding in SEN,* Fintan J. O'Regan
- *101 Essential Lists for SENCOs*, Kate Griffiths and Jo Haines
- *Coordinating Special Educational Needs: A Guide for the Early Years,* Damien Fitzgerald
- *Medical Conditions: A Guide for the Early Years,* Pam Dewis
- *Behavioural, Emotional and Social Difficulties: A Guide for the Early Years,* Janet Kay
- *Dyslexia 2nd Edition*, Gavin Reid
- *Dyspraxia 2nd Edition*, Geoff Brookes
- *Epilepsy*, Gill Parkinson

SENCO
at a glance

A Toolkit for Success

Linda Evans

continuum

Continuum International Publishing Group
The Tower Building   80 Maiden Lane, Suite 704
11 York Road   New York, NY 10038
London
SE1 7NX

www.continuumbooks.com

© Linda Evans 2007

All rights reserved. No part of this publication may be reproduced or transmitted in any form or by any means, electronic or mechanical, including photocopying (with the exception of the following pages which may be copied for use in the purchasing institution: 2, 5, 6, 8, 10, 13, 14, 16, 18, 19, 20, 22, 24–25, 29, 30–31, 34, 36, 37, 38, 41, 43, 44, 46, 47, 49, 50, 51, 54, 57, 60, 62, 64, 66), recording, or any information storage or retrieval system, without prior permission in writing from the publishers.

Linda Evans has asserted her right under the Copyright, Designs and Patents Act, 1988, to be identified as Author of this work.

British Library Cataloguing-in-Publication Data
A catalogue record for this book is available from the British Library.

ISBN: 9–780–82649–564–8 (paperback)

Library of Congress Cataloging-in-Publication Data

Evans, Linda, 1951 Oct. 3-
 SENCO at a glance : toolkit for success / Linda Evans.
   p. cm.
 Includes bibliographical references.
 ISBN-13: 978-0-8264-9564-8 (pbk.)
 ISBN-10: 0-8264-9564-8 (pbk.)
 1. Special education—Administration. 2. Children with disabilities—Education. I. Title.

 LC3969.E93 2007
 371.9'04—dc22

2007021950

Typeset by Free Range Book Design & Production Ltd
Printed and bound in Great Britain by Ashford Colour Press Ltd, Gosport, Hants.

Contents

Acknowledgements	vii
Introduction	ix

❶ SENCO as Manager — 1

Your Role and Status in the School	1
SENCO Role Audit	2
Provision Audit, Policy and Development Planning	4
Provision Audit	5
SEN/Inclusion Policy	6
SEN Development Plan	8
Provision Mapping by Year Group	10
Selection, Training and Monitoring of TAs/LSAs	12
Volunteer Recruitment Letter	13
Interviewing Candidates for a TA Post	14
Overview of Support Staff	16
Professional Needs Audit: SEN and Inclusion	18
Observing Group-work Support	20
Observing Classroom Support	21
Professional Development Review	22
Support for NQTs and Trainee Teachers	23
SEN Information Sheet	24
Demonstrating Effectiveness	28
Visual Representation of Data	29
Case Study: Primary	30

❷ Making an Impact on Teaching and Learning — 32

Every Child Matters	32
Helping Teachers to Develop Awareness of 'High Incidence' Needs	33
SEN Characteristics and Strategies	34
Specific Difficulties and Removing Barriers to Achievement	35
Sharing Information	36
Class Information Sheet	37
Support Strategies	38
Individual Behaviour Plan	41
Helping Teachers to Identify Children with SEN and Plan Accordingly	42
Cause For Concern Sheet	43
Differentiation Strategies	44

Targeting and Planning In-class Support	45
TA Support Planning Sheet	46
Working Together: Teacher and TA Partnership	47
Helping Teachers to Monitor and Record Progress	48
Record of Support (1)	49
Record of Support (2)	50
Monitoring for Inclusion	51

❸ Working With Other People: Professionals, Parents and Governors   52

Joint Working and Service-level Agreements	52
Service-level Agreement (Outreach)	54
Planning and Chairing Meetings	56
Record of Meeting	57
Parents	58
Parent/Carer Questionnaire	60
Pupil Participation	61
How am I Doing at School?	62
Governors	63
Report to Governors on SEN/Inclusion	64

In Conclusion   65

Glossary	66
Bibliography	67
Useful websites	68

Acknowledgements

My thanks go to:

- the many SENCOs and TAs I have worked with over the years, and particularly those who have kept me 'in the loop' recently while I have been writing this book.
- two friends and colleagues who have been more than generous in giving their time and sharing information with me – Sue Cunningham, who is Director of Inclusion at Castle High School and Visual Arts College, and Melanie Taylor, who is SENCO at Colley Lane Primary School. Both do a brilliant job in challenging circumstances.
- Dee Thomas, recently retired from SENCO-dom, who gave me invaluable feedback and advice, for which I am extremely grateful.
- Gill Minikin who provided some excellent examples of good practice at Chalfonts Community College during a NASEN conference I attended, and kindly gave permission for some of her material to be used in this book.

Introduction

If you are a SENCO (whether by choice or 'default'!), you have a very important job.

You are the champion of all the vulnerable children in your school. Yes, we all know that they're really every teacher's responsibility – but it's *you* who can be relied upon to understand their needs, recognize how to meet those needs, have the skill to put in place intervention programmes and help colleagues to make effective provision. It's you who has the responsibility of keeping track of pupils with special educational needs, making sure that they make progress and that they are included in all aspects of school life.

This book is for SENCOs who are passionate about doing a good job for children and young people with additional needs. It's about recognizing the breadth and depth of the role, managing the many aspects of the job, and 'keeping all the plates spinning'. I have written it for busy professionals who have little time for reading, so it is light on text and generous in giving you photocopiable pro forma to amend and use in any way that may improve your practice and save you time. In some cases, it will be the ideas, and possibly the form of words, that are useful rather than the actual format provided, but you are experts in 'personalization' and can alter templates to suit your own particular situation.

Wherever you are on the spectrum of professional performance, this book will help you to look at what you do, how well you're doing it and where you need to improve.

How to use this book: Throughout you will find titles of the photocopiable sheets **in bold**. These sheets are placed close to their first mention in the text for your use.

There is a glossary of acronyms and abbreviations on page 66.

1 SENCO as Manager

Your Role and Status in the School

The role of SENCO has changed significantly in recent years – and continues to do so. It's a role that is shaped by government strategy, workforce remodelling and ever more new initiatives, but is ultimately defined by each individual school and the needs of its pupils. The **SENCO role audit** (p. 2) will help you to audit your tasks throughout the year and define the extent of your role. This is useful for assessing your strengths and weaknesses, identifying areas for development/change and providing ammunition, if it's needed, for a higher position in the management pecking order of the school.

The Education and Skills Committee Report (July 2006) highlighted the fact that the DfES has placed a great deal of responsibility on the shoulders of SENCOs, but has not ensured:

'that SENCOs are always given the appropriate training – or the appropriate authority – to be able to undertake these significant responsibilities. Despite the recommendations in the Code of Practice that SENCOs should be part of a Senior Management Team this is often not the case.'

The Select Committee made several recommendations, including that 'the role of SENCO must reflect the central priority that SEN should hold within schools'.

To some extent, however, true 'status' cannot be conferred; an appropriate title and accompanying salary can give you a head start, but the respect of colleagues, pupils and parents has to be earned.

If you're dissatisfied with your status in school, ask yourself about the image you portray – as a 'specialist professional'. Do you attend phase/curriculum/pastoral meetings for example? If so, it conveys that 'SEN provision and inclusion is central to everything that goes on in the school – and as SENCO I need to be there'. Don't wait to be asked – approach the chairperson and explain why it's important for you to be involved and be part of the decision-making process. Be pro-active (see box 'Stepping up the Status', p. 3) – request regular meetings with the headteacher to keep him/her informed about your work, your successes and issues that arise. (The materials produced to support the National Quality Standards for SENCOs provide useful case studies showing how colleagues have used the standards as a basis for discussion with senior managers – see www.tda.gov.uk.)

SENCO Role Audit

Activity	% time spent/evidence/standard
Strategic management of SEN provision throughout the school, including policy writing and provision mapping	
Leading on the personalization agenda	
Preparation for and management of statutory assessments	
Organization and chairing of annual reviews (and termly?)	
Appointing and managing support staff (teaching and non-teaching) including deployment, training and monitoring	
Management of intervention programmes	
Writing/contributing to individual/group education plans (evaluating and renewing)	
Meeting with parents/carers; running workshops	
Preparing referrals and meeting with outside agencies	
Teaching: classes, groups, one-to-one	
Liaising with feeder/receiving schools and managing transition	
Tracking and reporting pupil progress	
Carrying out/organizing for assessments	
Budget and resource management; securing funding from the LA and other sources	
Acting as 'broker' to source a range of services for pupils	
Securing special arrangements for end of Key Stage tests and external exams	
Providing CPD for NQTs and other staff (planning and delivery)	
Reporting to governors	

> **Stepping up the status**
>
> - Adopt an appropriate title
> - Attend phase/curriculum/pastoral meetings – as appropriate
> - Be pro-active – produce a newsletter, share information in staff meetings
> - Deliver training
> - Have a noticeboard dedicated to SEN – either in the staffroom or on the intranet
> - Have regular meetings with the headteacher
> - Meet regularly with the governor with responsibility for SEN/inclusion
> - Be outward looking – attend regional and national conferences
> - Keep up to date with new developments and DfES (now DCSF) requirements
> - Look after your own CPD.
>
> Make sure you belong to the National Association for Special Educational Needs (NASEN); subscribe to professional journals to keep you up to date (for example, *SENCO Update* by Optimus Publishing, *Special Children* by Questions Publishing); go to the occasional conference and regular local network meetings – and READ! (One colleague does her professional reading each week while waiting for her children to come out of piano lessons – it's only an hour but it's regular and with practice you can scan through quite a lot in that time.)
>
> Sorry to be so non-PC, but do 'look the part' as well – a jacket beats a 'comfy cardy' every time!

If, in spite of your best efforts, your role continues to lack appropriate status, try getting the SEN governor onside as well as your School Improvement Partner, and don't be afraid of producing some of the wealth of documentation now available to support your bid; for example, The National Standards for Special Educational Needs Coordinators (TDA, 2006); the Report on Special Educational Needs from the House of Commons Education and Skills Select Committee (2006); various articles and information sheets from NASEN.

Provision Audit, Policy and Development Planning

Alongside the audit of your role, an audit of SEN provision in school will establish 'where you are' and provide a base from which to put together a Development Plan. A prompt sheet for your **Provision Audit** (p. 5) is provided.

A policy for SEN/Inclusion should set out the school's philosophy on identifying and providing for pupils with SEN, and describe how this is reflected in practice. Government strategy for SEN was outlined in *Removing Barriers to Achievement* (2004) and clarified what information should be included in a policy, namely:

- how you identify and make provision for children with SEN
- the facilities you have, including those which increase access for pupils who are disabled, including access to the curriculum
- how resources are allocated to and amongst pupils with SEN
- how you enable pupils with SEN to engage in activities of the school together with pupils with do not have SEN
- how the governing body evaluates the success of the school's work with pupils with SEN
- arrangements for dealing with complaints from parents.

Audit your SEN provision regularly and update the school's SEN/Inclusion policy.

A template for a school's **SEN/Inclusion Policy** (p. 6) is provided and there are other versions in abundance on the internet; but remember that your SEN policy must be *specific to your school*, so insert detail and amend subheadings as appropriate.

Provision for pupils with SEN is a matter for whole-school planning, but in most cases the SENCO will be the 'expert' in recognizing how targets relating to provision link into the 'big picture'. You need to be part of what is happening across the school and have access to the full range of information about pupil performance as well as being up to date about legislation and guidelines that impact on your work and planning.

Strategic planning is about formulating long-term objectives and devising a plan that will achieve them. Good planning will include details of:

- exactly what will be done, when and by whom
- what is needed in terms of resources (human and material) and costs
- how success will be measured
- how it will be evaluated, by whom and when
- how the evaluation will be used to inform future planning and action.

Provision Audit — photocopiable

Policy
- Is SEN/Inclusion policy up to date?
- Is it evaluated against practice?
- Does the SDP reflect SEN/inclusion objectives?
- Are objectives supported by detailed action plans?

Finance
- Is SEN funding transparent?
- Does budget planning focus on pupils' needs?
- Is there an evaluation of spending?

CPD
- Is there an ongoing programme of CPD for staff covering relevant areas of SEN?
- Is it evaluated?
- Are there reliable sources of information for staff to access easily?
- Are there areas of SEN expertise developing among the staff?

Provision
- Is there a broad range of provision to meet different needs?
- Is it allocated fairly and to best effect?
- Is it evaluated?
- Are there appropriate and up-to-date resources for pupils with SEN in all classes/departments?

Assessment
- Is there effective screening/testing to identify SEN?
- Is assessment information used to plan interventions/lessons?
- Is there analysis of information to feed into the SDP/SEF?

Monitoring
- Are there up-to-date records of all pupils with SEN?
- Is progress carefully monitored and targets reviewed regularly?
- Is there movement between sets and between SA/SA+?

Governors and parents
- Is there a named governor for SEN who meets regularly with the SENCO and takes an active interest in provision?
- Do governors receive regular reports on SEN provision and effectiveness?
- Are parents encouraged and helped to support their children?
- Are reports to parents given in a way that keeps them 'onside'?

Joint working
- Are there good working relationships with support agencies, EP and health professionals?

SEN/Inclusion Policy

photocopiable

The SEN/Inclusion Policy should provide basic information regarding the school's ethos, provision and practice.

1 Objectives of the policy
What is the school aiming to do in respect of vulnerable pupils: those with SEN, disabilities, in public care? (Refer to CoP, Removing Barriers to Achievement, Every Child Matters.)

2 Responsibility for coordination of inclusion and SEN provision
Who is responsible for coordinating the day-to-day provision of education for pupils on the Inclusion and/or SEN list? What are the respective roles and responsibilities of the headteacher, SEN governor, inclusion manager, SENCO and teachers in providing for pupils with additional and/or special educational needs?

3 Admission arrangements
What are the admission arrangements for pupils with SEN who do not have a statement if the arrangements differ from those for other pupils? (The CoP 1.33–1.36 covers school admissions and inclusion.)

4 Specialist SEN provision/facilities
Does the school specialize in any kind of provision for SEN or special units? What facilities does the school have for vulnerable pupils, pupils with SEN, including facilities that increase or assist access to the school by pupils who are disabled?

5 Identification and review of pupil needs
How are vulnerable pupils and those with SEN identified and their needs determined and reviewed?

6 Allocation of resources
How are resources allocated for different groups of pupils?

7 Access to the curriculum and out-of-school learning opportunities
What are the arrangements for ensuring access for pupils with SEN to a balanced and broadly based curriculum (including National Curriculum) and to the life of the school in broader terms?

8 Evaluating the effectiveness of provision
How will each type of provision for pupils with SEN be evaluated for its impact on pupil achievement and cost effectiveness?

9 Professional development
What arrangements are there for continuing professional development for staff, on a range of SEN issues and strategies for reducing barriers to achievement?

10 Multi-agency working
What use is made of other professionals, voluntary organizations, services and facilities from outside the school?

11 Working in partnership with parents
How does the school work in partnership with parents of vulnerable pupils and those with SEN/disabilities? What systems are in place for reporting to parents and involving them in reviews and planning? What are the arrangements for dealing with parental complaints about SEN provision?

12 Links with other schools
What links are there with other schools, including special schools and units? What provision is made for the transition of pupils between school and the next phase of education or work?

Success may be measured by a number of different outcomes – some easier to quantify than others, for example:

- improved attendance
- improved attainment (standardized tests, SATs, examples of work)
- fewer exclusions
- fewer incidences of bad behaviour
- fewer pupils on SA/SA+
- every child fully included in the curriculum and broader life of the school
- higher numbers attending study support sessions
- higher levels of parent involvement and support
- more positive pupil attitudes and higher self-esteem
- increased motivation/cooperation.

In order to quantify the school's goals, quantitative values need to be considered (sometimes in line with government strategy); for example, the goal could be a certain percentage of children achieving a certain NC level by the end of a key stage. In this way, everyone knows exactly what they are aiming for and can see whether the target is reached. The SENCO will be involved in analysing existing data and RAISEonline is expected to support this work (see national strategy documents: *Tracking for Success* DfES 1545-2005FLR-EN; *Effective Leadership: Ensuring the progress of pupils with SEN and/or disabilities* DfES 0140-2006 DOC-EN).

You might be looking at differences between cohorts and possible reasons for any dip in performance; the balance of boys/girls underperforming; the difference between subjects; whether cultural background/EAL is a contributory factor. In a school where low literacy levels are highlighted for example, with boys in particular achieving below L3 at KS2, the SENCO may draw up a **SEN Development Plan** (such as that on page 8). Ideally, the names of staff involved and money to be allocated from the SEN budget would be included.

Draw up an SEN Development Plan linked into the School Development Plan and transfer information into your provision mapping document (see pages 9 to 11). The SEN Development Plan should acknowledge the whole-school priorities.

SEN Development Plan

photocopiable

Trigger for action	35% achieving below L3 in Literacy at end KS2 (twice as many boys as girls)		
Target (what, by when)	Reduce % below L3 to 30% (2008), 25% (2009), 20% (2010)		
Strategies (what, who, when, where)	◆ In addition to current provision (see provision map*), to introduce Spirals Lang Dev programme in Rec (TA, 3x week) ◆ 'Books for boyz' project in KS2 (Reading buddies Mr H, Mrs D + TA) ◆ Workshop for parents of children in Y3 – how to help at home (SENCO) Spring term 4x 40 min ◆ INSET for whole staff (SENCO, NL Co-ord) 2x twilight		
Resources needed (costed)	◆ Spirals books + copying £60 ◆ New stock for 'books for boyz' £400 (PTA) ◆ Wellington Sq software + licence (£120) ◆ TA: 0.4 salary		
Success criteria (measurable/ demonstrable)	◆ Fewer referrals to SP & L ◆ Improved SAT results at KS2 ◆ Reduced imbalance boys/girls		
Evaluation (when, by whom)	◆ Individual staff to monitor on weekly basis SENCO to collate: ◆ Pupil progress records ◆ CPD evaluation sheets ◆ Attendance at Books for boyz project, comments from RBs and boys ◆ Attendance at parents workshops; comments		

* See page 10

Provision Mapping

This is a way of documenting the range of support provided in school and showing which pupils are allocated to different interventions. It can save a lot of time by reducing the number of individual plans needed, and is essential for effective monitoring by the SENCO (how can you keep on top of things if you aren't sure exactly what is being provided, when, by whom and for which pupils?).

Provision mapping should show in an accessible way, the various roles played by TAs and the different types of support they (and other staff) provide. For SENCOs in large schools (especially secondary), it can be useful to use some CPD time to ask support staff to list all the functions they undertake – there may well be pockets of 'informal support' that have sprung up in an ad hoc way without your knowledge. In one school for example, a TA had become particularly concerned about timekeeping and pupils' late arrival to lessons. She set up a 'clockwatch group' for the main offenders, introducing a competitive spirit to the matter of being on time – with recognition and rewards for the best timekeepers. This made a significant difference over time: to the teachers, who appreciated not having to 'start again' with explanations at the start of lessons, and to the pupils, who enjoyed the positive reinforcement and experienced a boost to their self-esteem.

This intervention was replicated with other groups – to good effect – but only came to light originally during an audit of provision where TAs worked in pairs to list all of the ways they supported pupils and staff.

Once completed, provision maps can be used to:

- conduct a regular audit of provision
- work out costs
- identify gaps in provision and repetitions
- assess effectiveness
- update the SEN development plan
- demonstrate accountability
- report to governors, parents, Ofsted
- focus on development of whole-school teaching and learning
- form the basis of IEPs (highlight the provision relevant to an individual and photocopy).

There are different ways of compiling provision maps – for example, by Year Group or CoP category (see **Provision Mapping by Year Group**, p. 10) – but SENCOs need to use a format that is useful to them in their particular school and situation. All additional provision should be listed (see p. 11 for examples) and the whole plan then needs to be populated with people to deliver. You can use a highlighted copy of this to show the provision accessed by an individual pupil, and use it to show parents, class teachers and so on.

Provision Mapping by Year Group

photocopiable

Year group	Provision/Resource	Individual/Group	Cost in time (per week)	Weeks to run/cost in £
All years	Differentiated curriculum planning, activities, input and outcome. Use of writing frames/keywords/ICT to support pupils with literacy difficulties. Setting: smaller/lower sets. Concessions for testing			
	SENCO/TA to support subject staff in planning and prep of modified materials. Rolling programme working within one subject area at a time for approx 8 weeks. Four subject areas per year		(1 x hour SENCO; 2h TA	32 weeks £
	In-class TA support focused on SEN pupils in subject areas		Equivalent of 7 x FT (TA)	All year £
	Lunchtime support/Homework club	Group (approx 15) 2 TAs	5 x 1h + 5 x 1h TA (10h)	All year £
	Individual behaviour programmes	Individual (4)	Approx 4 x 15 min (SENCO/pastoral team)	Continuous
Year 7	Paired reading with Yr 9 pupils during registration/tutor time (twice a week)	20 pairs (in 3 groups)	3 x 20 min SENCO; 3 x 20 min TA (1h +)	T1 & 2. Pupils may change over year according to progress
	Spelling group phonics programme during registration/tutor time	2 groups of 5	4 x 20 min TA (1h 20 min +)	All year. Pupils may change over year according to progress
	Intensive literacy support/mentoring (St, SA+). Withdrawn – following negotiation – from certain lessons	Individual (10 pupils)	10 x 25 min TA (5h +)	All year. Pupils may change dependent on progress
	Numeracy groups (during maths lessons)	2 groups of 4	8 x 25 mins with maths TA (4h +)	All year pupils change according to need
	Language/Social skills – small group during registration/tutor time	Group (6)	2 x 20 min TA (40 min +)	Term 1, 8 weeks
	Circle of Friends	Focus on individual	(Form Te and TA to support peer group) TA 20m/week	(Following initial PSHE lesson.) Continue as appropriate

SENCO AT A GLANCE
© LINDA EVANS (CONTINUUM 2007)

Examples of additional provision:

- One-to-one tuition (for example, Reading Recovery, precision teaching)
- One-to-one support (TA, reading buddy, mentor, counselling)
- Speech and language therapy
- Small-group intervention (language development, reading, writing, spelling, numeracy)
- Social skills/emotional literacy development
- Behaviour support
- Motor coordination programme
- Nurture group
- Circle of friends
- Lunchtime reading club
- After-school study support
- Keyboard skills
- Anger management
- Clockwatchers
- Peer tutoring
- Mentors
- Balance class (motor coordination)
- Parent workshop (for example, SHARE)
- Family literacy
- Story sacks
- In-class support
- Life skills group
- Vocational courses
- HI/VI support service input
- Special resources, hardware, software, large format books and so on.

(Check your own LA website for provision mapping guidance, or go to www.leics.gov.uk for a range of useful templates.)

Selection, Training and Monitoring of TAs/LSAs

The delivery of provision relies not only on you as SENCO but also, increasingly, on the teaching and non-teaching staff in your 'support team'. The selection and deployment of these people will be one of the most important aspects of your role because the calibre of your assistants and the quality of their work will impact directly on the effectiveness of provision.

> The calibre of your assistants and the quality of their work will impact directly on the effectiveness of provision.

Selection

You need to make sure that you recruit people who have appropriate personalities and attitudes, are intelligent and are willing to work hard. If they have experience in working alongside children with SEN and have relevant qualifications and knowledge, all the better, but knowledge can be learned and experience quite quickly gained. Negative attitudes and a reluctance to 'go the extra mile' are much more difficult to address. This is a difficult issue to overcome when time available for finding people (and pay offered to them) is limited. If you have a good system of recruiting voluntary helpers, these people can offer a wealth of support and constitute a 'pool' of people from which to recruit paid TAs. Encouraging parents, the 'active retired' and other members of the community to help out in classrooms and other areas of school gives you an opportunity to see how they respond to children, how quickly they pick up on systems and protocols, and how well they use their initiative.

See the example of a **Volunteer Recruitment Letter** opposite. The idea is to offer people as much choice as possible – to capitalize on their strengths and coax them in. Remember that you will need to apply appropriate 'safeguarding children' checks.

I can't pass over the opportunity here to say something about valuing your 'helpers'. I was once involved with a group of really marvellous, dedicated 'reading buddies' and never ceased to be amazed by how careless staff were about thanking them and making them feel valued. It matters. A lot! If you have good people and want to keep them on board, you have to work at it. Take an interest in them (it's a start to learn their name!); thank them every time; let them know about changes to the timetable, school closures and the like so that they don't arrive at school only to find that they're not needed/wanted; buy them chocolates at Christmas.

Interviewing candidates for TA posts can be time consuming, but it is important to do this as conscientiously as possible – it will save you time in the long run if you manage to make a good appointment. Don't be afraid to ask them to do a trial run with a group of children in the classroom, while you observe them; this is the best way to judge how well they relate and respond to pupils. Equally, you may decide to ask them to complete a short written assignment while waiting for their interview; this could be designing an IEP or considering how to help a certain child as described in a pen portrait – and can form the basis of the interview. Ideas for interview questions are outlined in **Interviewing Candidates for a TA Post** (p. 14). Think carefully about the venue for interviews – it should feel businesslike without being too daunting.

Volunteer Recruitment Letter   *photocopiable*

Dear Parent, Carer, Grandparent or other family member

We would like to invite you to join our team of volunteer helpers at school. We have a number of people who help out in different ways and offer valuable support to our teaching staff. If you think you could offer some time – on a regular basis, or 'now and then' – please complete this form and return it to the school office.

Yours,

Name:
Address:
Child's name and class:
Tel. number:

I am interested in (please tick):

- Helping groups of children in the classroom
- Listening to children read
- Reading to children
- Helping with numeracy
- Helping with ICT
- Putting up displays
- Making story sacks
- Helping children to tidy up after practical work
- Pairing up with a member of staff in the homework club/lunchtime study support
- Accompanying school outings
- Making masks and costumes
- Helping with school productions
- Helping with administration

I am regularly available on (please tick):

Monday:	morning	afternoon	evening
Tuesday:	morning	afternoon	evening
Wednesday:	morning	afternoon	evening
Thursday:	morning	afternoon	evening
Friday:	morning	afternoon	evening
Saturday:	morning	afternoon	evening
Sunday:	morning	afternoon	evening

I cannot promise a regular commitment but would be willing to help out on an occasional basis (please give details – e.g. once a term…) _____
_____

Interviewing Candidates for a TA Post

photocopiable

Always aim to conduct interviews with at least one colleague – possibly an experienced TA; the TA will bring a different perspective to the process and it's always helpful to discuss your ideas and feelings with someone rather than trying to 'go it alone'.

Remember that you want to give each candidate the opportunity to sell themselves as well as possible, so encourage them to do most of the talking. Here are some suggested question formats

1. We were pleased to receive your application … can you tell us why you applied for the job?
2. We noticed that you have worked at … Can you describe your role there and tell us about something that you are particularly proud of doing?
3. Can you tell us about your special qualities that will equip you well for this job?
4. We would like to hear about your experiences of … (choose from application, or refer to a specific part of the post being interviewed for – for example, working with children with speech and language/behaviour problems).
5. You have listed some courses that you've attended. Are there any areas you feel you need training in/would you be willing to go on a course suggested by the school?

Supporting children
6. Tell us how you would encourage a child to think for themselves/be independent in the lesson, rather than relying on your help.
7. How would you help a pupil who was a weak speller/reader/ had difficulty with handwriting?
8. Lots of children need extra help with numeracy – how would you support them in this lesson?
9. Helping children to stay on task and finish their work is often an important part of a TA's role – how can you help to motivate them?
10. Behaviour is an important aspect of good learning and teaching – how could you support the school's behaviour policy and keep a child 'on track'?

Supporting teachers
11. The relationship between teacher and TA is very important – what can you say about getting off to a good start and making sure that you establish a good working relationship with staff?
12. Confidentiality can be a sticky issue – for example, what are your feelings about talking to parents of children in the school about their progress/problems?
13. There are different ways of supporting a teacher other than helping children with their work – can you suggest other aspects of a TA's role? Are you willing to be flexible? Where would you draw the line?
14. What are your feelings about being involved in lesson planning, target setting and assessment?
15. How do you feel about attending review meetings?

Always give the candidate an opportunity to ask questions at the end of an interview and/or tell you anything that they feel you should know about but have not asked. You might also ask about where they see themselves in two years time – some may intend to embark on an HLTA or ITT course.

Prepare carefully for interviewing/recruiting teaching assistants.

Once TAs have been recruited, how you deploy, train, manage and monitor them will impact on their efficiency and the overall impact of SEN provision in the school.

Training

Make sure each TA has a detailed job description and invest some time in going through this as part of the induction process (it helps if teaching staff also have a copy, and understand the breadth of the TA role and their own responsibility in managing TAs). Producing an overview of support staff, with names, roles and times in school will help staff to see the 'big picture' of support in the school – and is also valuable to give to governors, Ofsted inspectors and HMI. For an example of this see the **Overview of Support Staff** (p. 16).

Some schools have handbooks for TAs, based on the staff handbook but with additional material relevant to the support role.

Material additional to the main staff handbook might include:

- information about IEPs, with examples
- an explanation of the pupil-review process and pro forma for TA input
- a list of special software, books and resources
- information on professional development opportunities and the system of review
- a glossary of terms and acronyms
- information on meeting a range of special needs and explanation of syndromes
- a list of outside agency personnel.

You don't have to take on the whole responsibility for delivering the training to TAs. Think about what other sources can offer: the local authority (support service staff, educational psychologists, Inclusion Partners); experienced TAs; speech and language therapists; school nurses; and colleagues from other (special) schools. In one cluster of schools, the SENCOs have become 'expert' in delivering training on one aspect of SEN and take it in turns to run twilight sessions on a rolling programme (dyslexia, autism, speech and language, behaviour and so on).

Overview of Support Staff

photocopiable

SEN and Inclusion Team

SENCO
Mrs T. Duffy

Learning Support Teachers	Teaching Assistants	Outside Agencies
Mr C. Hall Study Centre – F/T	Mrs Wembley (Mornings)	Miss Bell Sp. and lang. therapist
Miss Amey (M., Tu., W.)	Mrs Cole (M., Th., Fr.)	Mr Tudor EP
Mrs Vaughan Dyslexia (W., Th., F.)	Miss Tudor F/T	Mrs Moore Pupil Support Service
Mr Davison F/T	Mrs Frier F/T	
Mrs Stamp (M., W., Th.)		

Training for TAs needs to be:

- ongoing (to build up expertise; to cater for new recruits) and regularly audited
- little and often
- well planned
- varied in format – short presentations/video/reading/discussion/problem-solving
- active – not all sitting and listening
- relevant to the school, its pupils and TAs (INSET on specific syndromes, for example, will only be meaningful if there are pupils in school who have them). Ask TAs what they want/need – use the Professional Development Review form (p. 22)
- evaluated
- documented – as evidence of what has taken place; for audit purposes and as an aide-mémoire (brief notes/bullet points).

Make sure that any member of staff/TA who attends a course or conference outside school has the opportunity to disseminate their newfound learning to colleagues.

See the **Professional Needs Audit** (p. 18) as a template for seeking feedback from your support team.

Professional Needs Audit: SEN and Inclusion

photocopiable

Please complete and return to _____ by _____

Area	Preferred input: **A. INSET** **B. printed information** **C. advice from SENCO**	Priority 1 (low) – 10 (high)
Meeting needs of children with general learning difficulties		
Dyslexia, Dyspraxia, Dyscalculia		
Meeting needs of children with behavioural and emotional difficulties		
ADHD/ADD		
Meeting needs of children with speech and language difficulties		
Autism/Asperger's syndrome		
Hearing Impairment		
Visual Impairment		
Physical/Multi-sensory difficulties		
How to differentiate in the classroom		
Working in partnership with TAs		
Using ICT with pupils who have SEN		
Using the P scales		
Assessment for pupils with SEN		

Name:

Comments:

Monitoring

Monitoring the effectiveness of support staff is an essential part of ensuring quality provision but this is an aspect of the management role that many SENCOs find difficult to fit in. On a basic level, simply talking to staff about how a TA works in their classroom is a good start. This can be done incidentally in the staffroom and can provide useful feedback, but it's surprising how seldom this sort of informal monitoring is used. Remember to ask pupils as well; if a child is not 'getting on' with an assistant, the situation needs to be addressed.

Observing TAs, both in the classroom and while working with individuals and small groups outside the classroom, will give you a valuable opportunity to evaluate relationships and monitor the strategies being used. See the templates provided for **Observing Group Work Support** (p. 20) and **Observing Classroom Support** (p. 21). Complete the pro forma in good Ofsted fashion – that is, describe what you observe in terms of evidence of good practice, for example:

> TA's understanding of pupil's difficulties: *Mrs Timmins provided a selection of pens for Tom to choose from and different colours of paper. This was motivating for him and helped to offset some of the difficulties he has with writing.*

This activity also allows you to unobtrusively observe the teacher at work and monitor how well inclusive practice is established throughout the school (see Chapter 2).

Professional development reviews (PDRs) with TAs will provide opportunities to discuss your observations, suggest alternative/additional approaches and materials, and encourage the TA to reflect on and develop their own practice. Pairing up an inexperienced TA with a more experienced and skilled TA can be one of the best kinds of training. The pro forma provided for a **Professional Development Review** (p. 22) could be useful in helping a TA to prepare for a PDR.

Monitor the work of TAs and plan a programme of CPD based on your observations and professional development reviews.

Observing Group-work Support

photocopiable

TA:	Lesson:	Date:
Focus of group-work:		Number in group:

Evidence of:

Appropriate planning:

Preparation of resources:

TA's understanding of subject material:

TA's understanding of pupils' difficulties:

Appropriate and varied strategies used with pupils to maximize learning:

Effective use of ICT:

Good relationship with pupils:

Effective behaviour management:

Pupils being encouraged to be independent:

Effective monitoring of achievements (with reference to IEP):

Good response from pupils:

Effective communication/collaboration with teacher before/after lesson:

Smooth transition back to classroom:

Other positive observations:

Points for development:

Observing Classroom Support

photocopiable

| TA: | Lesson: | Date: |

Focus of support: general pupil support, specific group/pupil and so on.

Evidence of:

Prior planning, preparation of resources:

Effective behaviour management:

Encouragement and help for pupils to complete tasks:

Explanation/rewording/recap of objectives and/or instructions:

Pupils being encouraged to be independent, ask/answer questions:

Checking understanding:

Assistance given to pupils in recording:

Effective use of ICT:

Effective monitoring of achievements (with reference to IEP):

Good response from pupils:

Effective communication/collaboration with teacher:

Other positive observations:

Points for development:

Professional Development Review — photocopiable

Name: **Date:**

What I most enjoy about my job, and why.

What I least enjoy about my job, and why.

An example of a situation where I have had input and things have gone well. How this can be developed/done again.

How I know that I have made a difference.

An example of a situation where I have had input and things have not gone well. How this can be avoided, or the situation improved.

What I need to do to be more effective.

What I need others to do to help me be more effective.

I would benefit from some specific information/training on …

I would like to introduce the following practice/initiative over the next year.

Action points:

- ◆
- ◆
- ◆

Next review date:

Signed: _____ (Teaching assistant)

Signed: _____ (SENCO)

Support for NQTs and Trainee Teachers

An effective SENCO will try to support all colleagues, but providing information and guidance for trainee and newly qualified teachers is especially important. The amount of input on SEN issues received from their college course will vary, but is unlikely to be in any way comprehensive. Set up a short meeting with NQTs during their first week in school to alert them to pupils with SEN in their class/classes and go through essential information about relevant school systems. Preparing an 'at a glance' aide-mémoire can prove useful – see the **SEN Information Sheet** (p. 24) as an example of this. Being offered an 'SEN surgery' is something that all staff – but especially NQTs – value a lot. This might mean making yourself available in a set place, at a set time, every week, so that staff know that they can sit down and talk to you about a particular pupil, resources and/or approaches that may be useful. You won't be able to wave a magic wand, but sometimes just being able to share concerns and be cautioned that there is no quick-fix solution can be very reassuring for inexperienced teachers.

Collect together useful books, website addresses and other resources and make them accessible to colleagues.

Definitions

The 'SEN' acronym has come to mean 'all things to all men', so a good place to start may be with the official definition of special needs and the categories specified in the Code of Practice. Many schools have developed their own terminology for pupils who have additional needs and this will have to be clearly explained to new staff.

Provide a glossary of acronyms and specialist terminology for all new staff. You may wish to use the glossary at the back of this book.

SEN Information Sheet — photocopiable

Definition of SEN

Children have special educational needs if they have *a learning difficulty or disability which calls for special educational provision* to be made for them. 'Special educational provision' is additional to, or different from, the educational provision made generally for children of the same age in local schools. In the majority of cases, the provision is made within a child's local mainstream school. Special schools provide for children with more complex and severe needs.

Types of SEN

Cognition and Learning	Behavioural, Emotional and Social Difficulties (BESD)	Communication and Interaction	Sensory and/or physical
Specific learning difficulties (SpLD) e.g. Dyslexia, Dyscalculia, Dyspraxia Moderate Learning Difficulties (MLD), sometimes referred to as Global Learning Delay Severe Learning Difficulties (SLD) Profound and Multiple Learning Difficulties (PMLD)	Behavioural and emotional difficulties Attention-Deficit Disorder (ADD) Attention-Deficit Hyperactivity Disorder (ADHD)	Speech and language difficulties Autistic Spectrum Disorders (ASD) Asperger's Syndrome	Hearing Impairment (HI) Visual Impairment (VI) Multi-sensory impairment Physical Difficulties (PD)

Code of Practice for Special Educational Needs

The CoP (DfES 2001) states that children with special educational needs should:

- have their needs met, normally in a mainstream school or setting.
- be offered full access to a broad, balanced and relevant education (including an appropriate curriculum for the Foundation Stage, and the National Curriculum).

The CoP also states that parents have a vital role to play in supporting their child's education, and that the views of the child should be sought and taken into account.
(See CoP at 4:27 for early years, 5:50 for primary and 6:58 for secondary guidance.)

The CoP sets out a continuum of intervention:

- *School/early years Action*: a child is identified as needing extra support and this is provided within the school.
- *School/early years Action Plus*: after a period of extra support, the school seeks advice/support from external agencies such as the Learning Support Service, a Speech and Language Therapist or Behaviour Support Team. An Individual Education Plan (IEP) is formulated.

In a minority of cases, pupils are assessed by a multi-disciplinary team on behalf of the local education authority, whose officers then decide whether or not to issue a *Statement of SEN*. This is a legally binding document which details the child's needs and specifies the resources to be provided. It is reviewed at least once a year.

SEN Information Sheet (continued) — photocopiable

Individual Education Plans

An IEP describes actions to be taken, over and above the day-to-day differentiation in the class, in order to enable a child to make progress. (Group education plans (GEPs) are drawn up where several children in the class have common targets for which common strategies are appropriate.) The best IEPs are planning, teaching and reviewing tools that include two or three SMART targets (Specific, Measurable, Achievable, Relevant and Timed). There should be details of strategies for meeting these, clear success criteria and a review date. An IEP or GEP should therefore always state *what* is to be done, *when* it will happen and be reviewed, and *who* will be involved.

Learning styles

Visual–auditory–kinaesthetic (VAK)

By using multi-sensory teaching approaches and encouraging pupils to employ a wide range of learning styles, teachers can maximize learning potential.

Visual:	symbol support, classroom display, posters, pictures, video, mind maps, diagrams, graphs, pictograms, highlighting text, using colour, illustrations, interactive whiteboards, computer software
Auditory:	listening to teacher/classmates/tapes/audio output from computer; group discussion, debate, talking partners, interviewing, oral feedback; using background music
Kinaesthetic:	touching, making, manipulating, building, modelling, conducting practical investigations, preparing food

It is important to review newly learned material and provide plenty of opportunity to consolidate new skills when working with children who have learning difficulties.

Attitudes to pupils with SEN

The attitudes of staff with regard to teaching children with special educational needs are the single, most important factor in making good provision. Where teachers are sensitive to individual needs, accept diversity and take on board the responsibility for ensuring that every child achieves, they will succeed in creating a supportive and inclusive learning environment. It is important that NQTs understand the ethos of the school with regard to inclusion, as well as the government's stance, and accept the responsibility for every child in their class making appropriate progress.

It can be difficult for inexperienced teachers to know how much to expect from children with SEN, and SENCOs can be of valuable assistance here. Having low expectations and 'feeling sorry' for a child is not the answer, but neither, usually, is a belief that if 'he just tried harder' he could achieve as much as everyone else. IEPs can be helpful in guiding a teacher's expectations. Every teacher should be aware of current targets for the children they teach – and how they can contribute to the child's success in meeting those targets. This will become second nature for teachers in primary schools who will usually work alongside the SENCO in drawing up an IEP, but may seem less obvious for subject teachers in secondary schools.

Explain how IEPs are drawn up and used in your school. Provide NQTs and trainees with opportunities to observe children with special needs, and see how they respond to effective teaching, both in whole-class and in small-group/individual situations.

Knowledge of particular needs

Detailed knowledge of syndromes and conditions will be acquired over time, as and when teachers come into contact with particular children, but an awareness of the more common 'high incidence' needs will enable NQTs to support children's learning regardless of which 'label' is appropriate.

It is always a mistake however, to 'put children in boxes'. Instead, encourage teachers to look at what pupils can do, what they find difficult and try out as many different strategies as possible to help them achieve success (remembering to ask the pupils themselves – they often know exactly what they need).

Provide practical information on, for example, autism, dyslexia, dyspraxia, global learning difficulties, glue ear, speech and language difficulties.

Creating an inclusive learning environment

This is about more than the physical environment, of course, though consideration of furniture and furnishings, wall displays, storage of equipment and so on can have an important bearing on how comfortable children are in a classroom, how well they can access resources and, ultimately, how well they 'perform'. Emphasize that the creation of a truly inclusive learning environment involves reassuring pupils that:

- they are allowed to 'get it wrong' sometimes
- they can take risks
- they can ask for help (and receive it)
- they will be commended for effort as well as achievement
- different types of ability are valued
- different learning styles are acknowledged and catered for.

In general, what is good practice for teaching pupils with SEN is good for *all* children, but there will be times when specific action is required to ensure access to learning for some pupils and effective differentiation will be needed to achieve this.

Help NQTs to develop a range of differentiation strategies and make sure that they are familiar with P levels and how to use them in planning for pupils with more significant difficulties.

Demonstrating Effectiveness

Having implemented a range of interventions and delivered training to improve school-wide inclusive practice, you will want to asses how well everything is working and produce some documentation to share with SMT, governors, Ofsted and so on. Children aren't machines – you can't improve some process on the production line and expect to see immediate and tangible results – it's more complicated than that. Nevertheless, we have to be able to show that what we are doing is working and there are a number of ways to do this. The most effective way of demonstrating success within SEN provision is to build up a portfolio of evidence that includes a mixture of quantitative and qualitative material. This might include:

> *We have to be able to show that what we are doing is working and there are a number of ways to do this.*

- reading tests/keyword tests/SATs levels (before-and-after scores/amount of progress made over twelve months/one key stage/whole secondary phase)
- screening information (for example, Dyslexia screener) showing progress over time
- P Scale descriptors
- attendance graphs
- behaviour measures
- examples of pupils' work
- letters of thanks from parents
- records of achievement
- teacher/parent/pupil voices (possibly responses to questionnaires)
- case studies (of individual pupils and/or specific projects).

It's a good idea to keep in your head the question 'How do you know that what you are doing is effective? What is the evidence?' Test this out in terms of everything on your provision map. Are the small groups having a positive effect – how do you know? Is Reading Recovery more effective than phonics groups? Do the parent workshops actually achieve anything? This information will then feed into your SEF, and ultimately contribute to the school SEF.

For example, if you tick the 'Yes' box to say that 'identification procedures for pupils with SEN are in place and used by all staff', what is your evidence to show that this is actually happening?

Your response might be: 'Provision map; liaison with feeder schools; cause for concern forms; parent and pupil questionnaires.'

When you have collected evidence, how you present it to people is very important. Reams and reams of test scores for example are not easy to digest – you need to make sense of that sort of data for the reader. Visual representation of data is usually easier to understand – and makes more of an impact than columns of figures. There will be software in school to help with this – Microsoft Excel, for example, will convert data into graphs and bar charts at the touch of a button. There are some examples of presentation styles in the sheet **Visual Representation of Data** (opposite) and in the **Case Study: Primary** (p. 30).

Plan 'data collection' points throughout the school year. Use admin support or a TA to help you.

Visual Representation of Data   photocopiable

Example 1

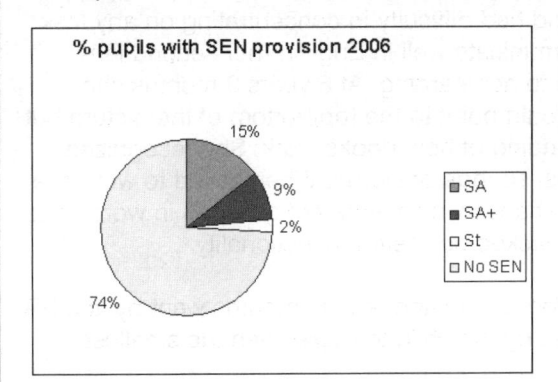

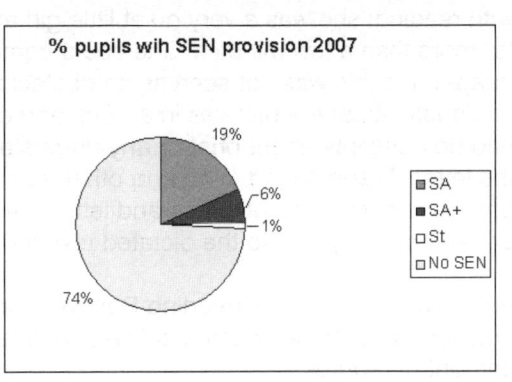

% pupils with SEN provision 2006
- 15% SA
- 9% SA+
- 2% St
- 74% No SEN

% pupils wih SEN provision 2007
- 19% SA
- 6% SA+
- 1% St
- 74% No SEN

Example 2

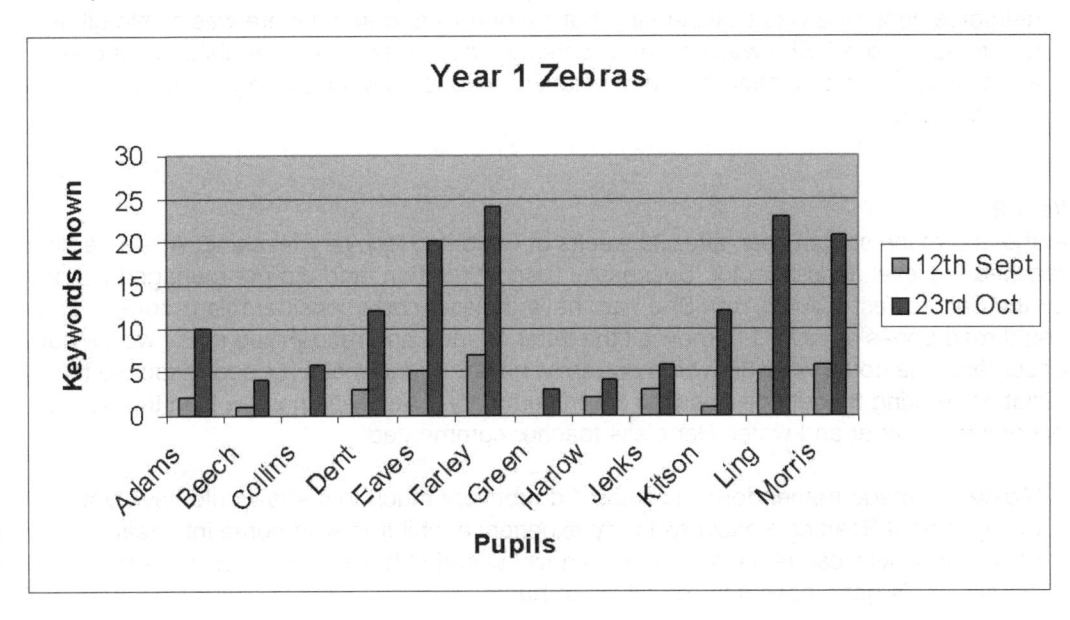

Year 1 Zebras

Bar chart showing Keywords known (0–30) for pupils Adams, Beech, Collins, Dent, Eaves, Farley, Green, Harlow, Jenks, Kitson, Ling, Morris on 12th Sept and 23rd Oct.

Example 3

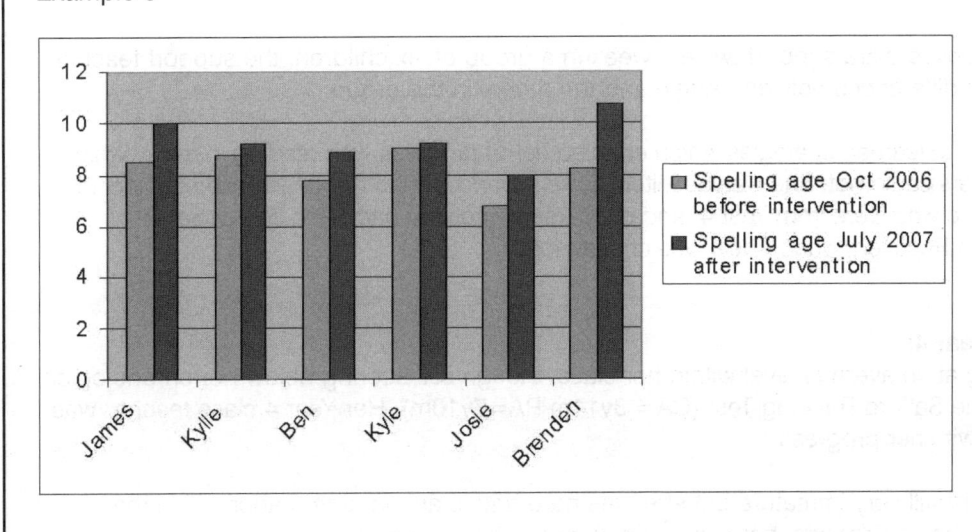

Bar chart (0–12) for pupils James, Kylie, Ben, Kyle, Josie, Brenden comparing:
- Spelling age Oct 2006 before intervention
- Spelling age July 2007 after intervention

Case Study: Primary

photocopiable

Adele began school with a very low baseline and in Year 1 had not really made any start with reading; she was a very quiet little girl and had difficulty in concentrating on any task for more than a few minutes. She could communicate well in English (her second language) and this was not seen as an obstacle to her learning. At 6 years 3 months she could talk about the pictures in a book and could point to the top/bottom of the picture but had no concepts about print or any understanding of how books work. She recognized the letter 'A' and sound 'a' but no other letters, sounds or words. When asked to write she produced a few lines of letters and letter-like shapes which were not grouped in word units or related in any way to the dictated text and lacked consistent directionality.

Adele was put onto the Reading Recovery programme and, as the months went by, the RR teacher realized how much effort was required by the child to make even the smallest amount of progress:

> 'It was very hard work and progress was very, very slow. She needed lots and lots of re-inforcement. She was exasperating but every now and again there was a little glimmer to spur me on. She was probably working harder than any other child in the class at that time – just becoming aware of what was expected of her, trying to make sense of everything.'

Year 2:
at the end of the school year, after 30 weeks of Reading Recovery teaching, Adele had not reached the level necessary for 'Successful Discontinuation' and did not manage to score on the Salford Test (CA=7y1m). She had, nevertheless made considerable progress; she could read books at Level 11, knew all the letter sounds and recognized many words out of context. She could write 36 words correctly, unaided, and make a good response to dictation, scoring 31 out of a possible 37. In summary, Adele was now well on the way to becoming a reader and writer. Her class teacher commented:

> 'Adele has made tremendous progress. I doubt very much that she would have got going without Reading Recovery. In my experience, children who come into Year 2 with so few skills can really get stuck. I know I wouldn't have moved her on as much as this. She's got a base now, on which to build.'

Year 3:
Adele received extra support twice a week in a group of six children; the support teacher noted the differences between Adele and the others in the group:

> 'Adele had learned strategies which enabled her to progress with reading in a way which the others could not. She was definitely more advanced than the other children – including some who were from Year 4, and of course some who had been 'too good' for Reading Recovery when Adele was chosen for it.'

End of Year 4:
achieving at an average level within her class, though still scoring below her chronological age on the Salford Reading Test (CA= 8y11m RA=7y10m). Her Year 4 class teacher was pleased with her progress:

> 'Adele is still very immature but she tries hard and is an average reader within the class. She gets on with her work – I'm very positive about her.'

Case Study: Primary (continued) *photocopiable*

Year 5: (aged 9 years 4 months)
Adele achieved a Standardized Score of 101 on the LEA Reading Screening (NFER) which placed her ahead of 50 per cent of the children in her class. Adele is an example of a child who was a negative statistic in terms of 'Successful Discontinuation'. Yet everyone involved with Adele judged the programme to have been very successful; it laid the foundations for her reading development in a way which otherwise would not have been achieved.

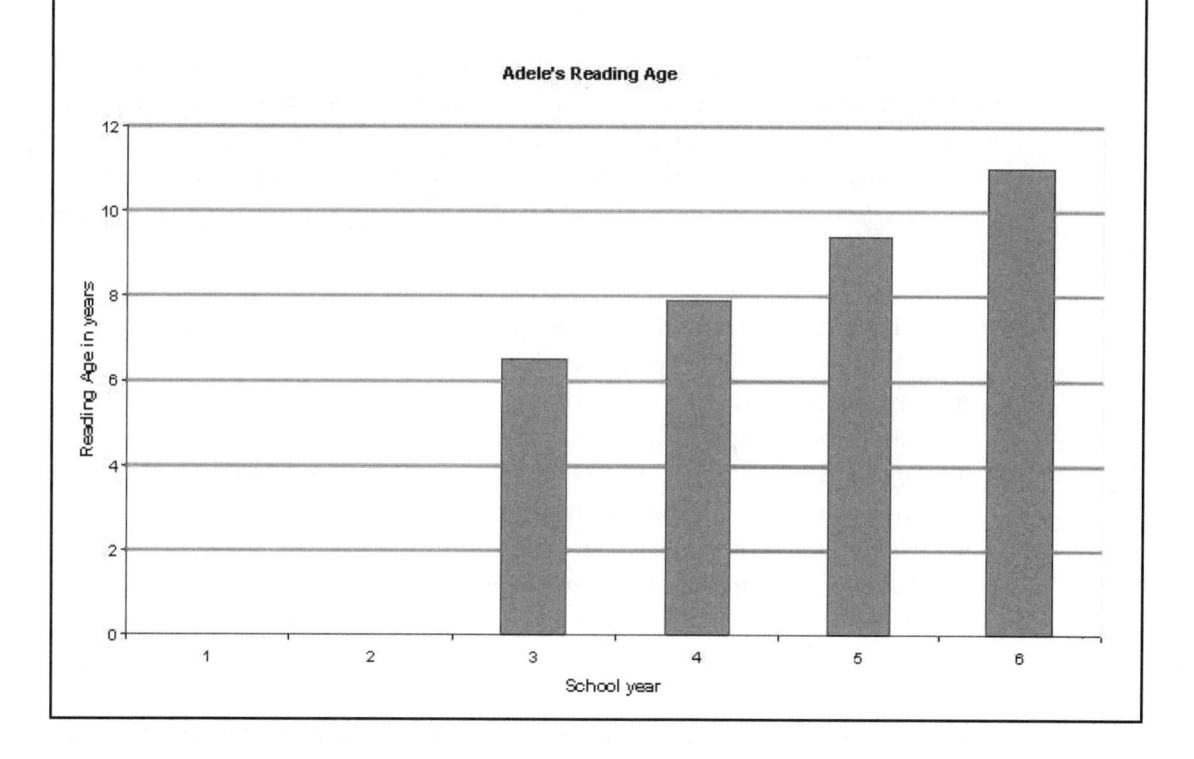

Adele's Reading Age

(Bar chart showing Reading Age in years vs School year: Year 3 ≈ 6.5, Year 4 ≈ 7.9, Year 5 ≈ 9.3, Year 6 ≈ 11.)

2 Making an Impact on Teaching and Learning

Every Child Matters

The SENCO role is now about much more than identifying children's needs and putting in place interventions to address them. Recent legislation and guidance means that the SENCO has to be much more powerful in influencing teaching and learning throughout the school and in helping to secure the five ECM outcomes. Some specific examples of SENCO action in this respect are outlined below.

- *Being healthy*: arranges for PE adviser to deliver training to staff on activities suitable for pupils with mobility difficulties
- *Staying safe*: sets up a Circle of Friends for pupil with Asperger's syndrome to support him and minimize bullying
- *Enjoying and achieving*: ensures that staff use ICT in lessons to give pupils alternate means of communicating and recording achievement
- *Making a positive contribution*: trains and supports peer tutors
- *Achieving economic and social well-being*: runs a lunchtime 'money club' to ensure that pupils develop practical numeracy skills and understand about spending and budgeting.

These outcomes will have to be incorporated into every teacher's planning of course, and the SENCO can play a valuable role in supporting colleagues in their efforts to provide appropriately for pupils with SEN. This will involve making sure that teachers:

- have a good awareness of 'high incidence' needs and use strategies to support pupils in their lessons (for example, dyslexia, ADHD, global learning difficulties)
- know about the specific difficulties experienced by individual children and how to remove barriers to achievement (for example, providing accessible switches for a child with cerebral palsy)
- can identify which children need additional support
- can set appropriate learning objectives, plan accordingly, be flexible
- can deploy and liaise with TAs to good effect
- can monitor and record progress, even when very slight.

Let's not underestimate the size of this task! In order to get anywhere with it, you will need to have the status/authority in school (see p. 1); excellent communication and interpersonal skills; knowledge of SENs and effective strategies to meet those needs; resources, time and good time management. You are probably already doing a lot to support teachers in the areas outlined above; this section offers ideas to help you develop and improve your practice.

Helping Teachers to Develop a Good Awareness of 'High Incidence' Needs

Provide Information

There is no shortage of information on different types of SEN and strategies for teachers to adopt, but beware of some of the more eccentric websites (especially from outside the UK) and rely instead on national organizations such as the British Dyslexia Association, umbrella bodies such as OAASIS, or reliable sources such as East and Evans (see Bibliography). Make sure that there is information readily available to staff – in the staffroom, SENCO room and/or on the intranet. Use the noticeboard to highlight relevant TV programmes that come up from time to time.

Make Colleagues Think About the Information and How to Use It

It is a straightforward process to source and copy concise information to distribute to teachers, but ensuring that they read it is another matter. If you can secure some CPD time – a twilight session or INSET day, to involve them in some sort of activity around using the information you give – you'll find that it is all the more meaningful to them.

See the teacher's activity **SEN Characteristics and Strategies** (p. 34): copy this sheet, cut it up into individual boxes and ask colleagues to assemble these 'correctly'. They will realize that there is a great deal of overlap in terms of both 'characteristics' and 'strategies' – what is good practice for one child with special needs, tends to be useful for others too. Teachers who are receptive to good practical guidance, soon build up a repertoire of SEN-friendly strategies that become embedded in their everyday practice.

This activity could be followed up by asking staff to contribute to a discussion on 'what works for them' with particular pupils, and whether whole-school strategies are effective in supporting individuals (teachers and pupils). TAs can talk about good practice from their point of view and describe successful lessons they have supported.

Provide good models

Use DVDs to demonstrate and discuss strategies (the national strategy material includes useful sequences of teachers working with pupils who have SEN), or give colleagues opportunities to see good practice in other classrooms – either within the school or elsewhere. This isn't always easy of course: no teacher welcomes the suggestion that someone else is 'doing it' better than they are, but watching other people teach is possibly the best way of helping us to reflect on and develop our own practice. In schools where lesson observation – of all kinds, for all reasons – is accepted as the norm, there won't be a problem with this type of CPD.

SEN Characteristics and Strategies

photocopiable

Special Educational Need	Characteristics	Strategies
Attention Deficit Disorder – with or without hyperactivity	◆ has difficulty following instructions and completing tasks ◆ easily distracted by noise, movement of others ◆ can't stop talking, interrupts others, calls out ◆ acts impulsively without thinking about the consequences	◆ keep instructions simple – the one sentence rule ◆ make eye contact and use the pupil's name when speaking to him ◆ sit the pupil away from obvious distractions ◆ provide clear routines and rules, rehearse them regularly ◆ break up activities, provide variety
Autistic Spectrum Disorder	◆ may experience high levels of stress and anxiety when routines are changed ◆ may have a literal understanding of language ◆ more often interested in objects rather than people ◆ may be sensitive to light, sound, touch or smell	◆ give a timetable for each day ◆ warn the pupil about changes to usual routine ◆ avoid using too much eye contact as it can cause distress ◆ use simple clear language; avoid using metaphor and sarcasm ◆ provide a distraction-free area to work
Down's Syndrome	◆ takes longer to learn and consolidate new skills ◆ limited concentration ◆ has difficulties with thinking, reasoning, sequencing ◆ has better social than academic skills ◆ may have some sight, hearing, respiratory and heart problems	◆ use simple, familiar language ◆ give time for information to be processed ◆ break lesson up into a series of shorter, varied tasks ◆ accept a variety of ways of recording work, e.g. use drawings, diagrams, photos, video ◆ appoint a work buddy
Dyslexia	◆ needs help with organization ◆ finds reading difficult ◆ has more ability than written work suggests ◆ confuses letter shapes – for example, b/d/p/q ◆ spelling can be bizarre	◆ allow extra time for completion of work ◆ acknowledge the effort required to complete a piece of writing ◆ help pupil to organize himself and his work (teach study skills) ◆ make use of ICT

Specific Difficulties and Removing Barriers to Achievement

Increasingly, schools are using provision mapping and personalized learning initiatives to set targets and record outcomes for all pupils, including those with SEN. In order to meet individual needs however, teachers need to have a certain amount of information about pupils and it is the SENCO's job to present this in a way that is concise and accessible.

> At Chalfonts Community College, staff found that IEPs were not manageable, but the provision map did not give enough information on individual pupils. A new system was devised whereby each teacher was given concise information about pupils with SEN in a class. See the **Pupil Information Sheet** and **Class Information Sheet** (pp. 35–36).
>
> Each pupil's details are entered into one cell of an Excel spreadsheet on the school's shared drive from where teachers can extract the information, sort it into classes, sets and so on. This information can be used to differentiate appropriately, with reference to the **Support Strategies** (see sheet provided as an example, p. 38) also listed on the shared drive and is available for cutting and pasting into more detailed IEPs if appropriate, with subject-specific targets.
>
> This information can be adapted for use in pupil reviews, reports and so on cutting down on SEN bureaucracy.

For pupils with significant needs, however, an Individual Education/Behaviour Plan (IEP/BP) can be a useful tool. Properly designed and implemented, it provides valuable guidance for professionals working with a child (particularly where individual/small group intervention is in place) and reassurance to parents/carers that the school is doing its job properly. It also fulfils an important review and evaluation role.

Sharing Information
photocopiable

1. ◆ S: Statement for students with the greatest needs. There is a legal agreement to provide a specified amount of support to meet agreed targets. These students have the highest priority for support.
   ◆ SA+: School Action Plus. These students' needs are so great that they need help from other professionals, such as a specialist teacher, an educational psychologist or an education welfare officer, as well as different ways of teaching or extra resources.
   ◆ SA: School Action. These are students who need different ways of teaching or extra resources (for example, different worksheets or LSA support in some lessons).
   ◆ A few students don't have a stage next to their name. These students are not officially on the SEN Register, so they won't have full IEPs, but teachers need to follow the advice given in their summary.

2. For each category of Special Educational Needs, there is a set of Suggested Strategies for class teachers to use. Using these strategies will help the student to make progress in a way that is manageable for the class teacher.

3. Students of average ability have a Reading Age the same as their chronological age. A student with a Reading Age below 9 yrs 6 months may need differentiated texts, or help with reading in lessons.

4. Students with a Spelling Age below 9 yrs will find it difficult to write independently unless the have a clear outline of what they have to do and a list of spellings they might need.

5. Students who write less than 75 words in 5 minutes may have difficulty keeping up in an average class.

> **[Pupils name]**
> _____ SEN Stage: School Action[1]. SEN Categories: Learning. Reading. Spelling[2]. Reading Age: 9.03[3], Spelling Age: 8.10[4], Writing Speed (wds in 5 mins): Copying: 85, Free Writing: 121[5]. VR: 85[6]. KS2 SATs: Eng: 3, Ma: 4, Sci: 4[7]. Enjoys fishing. Reading now more fluent and starting to self-correct but still needs lots of practice. Has LSA for individual reading each week. Needs to read something he enjoys at home. Spelling difficulties mean he still needs short, clear tasks with key words given. Needs to record own homework in full. Needs careful seating plan and close monitoring to improve concentration. Good oral participation. Has difficulty copying accurately so may need carbon copy from peer. May need extra time for exams[8].

6. This is the score from the Buckinghamshire Verbal Reasoning test (11+). The minimum score for a grammar school place is 121. A score of 0 means that they weren't entered for the test. The College thinks that students with a score of over 100 should get five GCSEs at Grades A–C. The College considers that students with a score of over 110 are 'gifted and talented'.

7. These are the National Curriculum tests (Standard Assessment Tests). Students do these tests in Year 6 (Key Stage 2 tests) and Year 9 (Key Stage 3 tests). Average attainment is Level 4 at KS2 and Level 5 or 6 at KS3.

8. The exam boards have strict criteria. They will only allow concessions if there is sufficient evidence of need, and if the concessions requested are the student's usual way of working. Spelling is judged by intelligibility, not just by accuracy.

Adapted from a system used at The Chalfonts Community College.

Class Information Sheet

photocopiable

Year 9

Pupil	Set	CoP and assessment information; main areas of difficulty; pointers for teachers
Jones, K.	S5	**SA+, Behaviour (ADHD) Concentration Organization** Reading Age 9.07, Spelling Age 10.08, KS2 SATs: Eng: Abs, Ma: 3, Sci: 3, VR: 91. Has great difficulty complying with class norms but has shown improvement in Year 8. Member of social skills group. Needs to be encouraged to see possible consequences of behaviour. Extreme organizational difficulties – keeps all books and work in LS Department. Does homework in LS Dept after school. Takes Ritalin. Must be allowed to leave class to use the toilet. Responds well to firm boundaries and praise. Any concerns please pass to LS Department.
Lenon, P.	S5	**SA–, Behaviour Spelling** Reading Age 11.08, Spelling Age 11.08, KS2 SATs: Eng: 3, Ma: 3, Sci: 4, VR: 93. Behaviour is often inappropriate and concentration is lacking, leading to under achievement. Needs clear firm boundaries for behaviour, and targets for work that should be achieved. Must be encouraged to have a more positive attitude to school work.
Mattis, C.	S6	**SA, Spelling Reading** Reading Age 10.03, Spelling Age 9.04, KS2 SATs: Eng: 3, Ma: 3, Sci: 4, VR: 87. Sometimes under stress. Vulnerable within school – victim of some bullying. Handwriting and presentation poor, needs to be reminded to think about this. May help if some work could be done on a word processor. Usually asks for help and appreciates support. Need to check that she tries the work herself first. Very cooperative. Must wear glasses. Had small-group teaching for spelling/literacy with LS Department 2002.
Jones, S.	S8	**SA–, Concentration Attendance** Reading Age 10.08, Spelling Age 9.10, KS2 SATs: Eng: 3, Ma: 4, Sci: 4, VR: 90. Some concerns about underachievement. Progress hampered by poor attendance – Year 8, 77%. Needs to be 95%. Reading and Spelling Age scores reflect underachievement. She has previously scored much better in these tasks.
Tonks, M.	S6	**SA, Behaviour Attendance** Reading Age 11.06+, Spelling 12.06, KS2 SATs: Eng: 4, Ma: 4, Sci: 5, VR: 96. Behaviour has deteriorated in recent months. Needs very clear guidelines for appropriate behaviour. Often seeks attention in an inappropriate manner and needs support to move away from this negative attitude. Responds well when he receives appropriate praise. Attendance also needs to improve – Year 8, 79%. Needs to aim for at least 90%. In Year 8 has almost continually been on report.
Trent, S.	S6	**SA–, Attendance Spelling** Reading Age 11.06+, Spelling Age 9.06, KS2 SATs: Eng: 4, Ma: 4, Sci: 4, VR: 94. Keen to do well and responds well to positive reinforcement. Reading skills have improved but needs to read regularly to maintain standard. Had LS teaching in Year 8. Spelling still causes difficulties and will require key words for written tasks. Must proofread her work. Use of IT and spell checker may help with this. Attendance causes concern, 80% in Year 8. Target needs to be 95%.

Adapted from a system used at The Chalfonts Community College.

Support Strategies

photocopiable

SEN Category:	Reading difficulties
Target:	To be able to read and understand curriculum texts

Responsibility	Suggested strategies
LS Dept	◆ (For neediest students) Specialist individual or small-group teaching: structured programme to develop phonological ability. ◆ Exam concessions put in place where appropriate. ◆ LS base available at lunchtimes for support. ◆ Some in-class LSA support.
Subject teachers	◆ Hear student read (discretely if necessary) to gauge accessibility of texts. ◆ Provide easier texts if necessary – short sentences, plenty of pictures, difficult words explained. ◆ Try to give reading practice in every lesson. ◆ Where necessary, provide other means of accessing text (for example, text read aloud in class; pair student with a more able peer; put texts on tape). ◆ Discuss subject-specific keywords, have these displayed in classroom (not in capitals) and draw attention to written form during discussion. ◆ On board, write large and clearly. ◆ Have on the board only what's needed for that lesson. ◆ Consider using different colours for alternate lines of writing on board (makes it easier for students to find the right place). ◆ Use pictures, videos and role-plays – not just reading.
Student	◆ I will read at home for at least 15 mins at least four times a week. ◆ I will ask the teacher or an LSA to help me read any words I find difficult in class. ◆ When I read, I will think about what I am reading and try to pick out the main ideas. ◆ I will attend any extra reading practice which is set up for me.

Adapted from a system used at The Chalfonts Community College.

In evaluating your system of IEP/BPs consider whether:

- they describe meaningful objectives, with success criteria detailed as SMART targets (specific, measurable, achievable, relevant, timed)
- each one has a focus rather than attempting to cover diverse needs – with no more than three or four targets that are easy to understand
- the strategies to be used are clearly laid out, with details of who will do what, when and where
- they include strategies for class/subject teachers as well as details of specific interventions in small-group or one-to-one sessions
- they are actually read and used by all staff working with the pupil
- the pupil and their parents/carers are involved in the writing and evaluation of the IEP wherever possible.

An IEP describes actions to be taken, over and above the day-to-day differentiation in the class, in order to enable a child to make progress. The whole point of it is that it is *individual* – matched to a specific child's needs. If you use software or published schemes to help with this (and they do save a lot of time), make sure that you amend appropriately to get a 'good fit'. (Group education plans (GEPs) can be useful where several children in the class have common targets for which common strategies are appropriate.) Targets should be described in jargon-free language and be clear to all concerned – not least the pupils themselves, who should be able to say 'Today I hit one of my targets … I got to school on time/ spelled all ten target words correctly/asked a question in class.'

There should be details of strategies for meeting these targets and approaches/resources/materials/software to be used. Clear success criteria and a review date will help all concerned to decide what is working – and what is not.

> Individual Plans should be working documents, relevant to all staff working with the student and constantly at hand.

Individual Plans should be working documents, relevant to all staff working with the student and constantly at hand, not neatly filed away in a drawer: if it is pristine, the chances are that no one is reading and using it, but if it is dog-eared, with notes scribbled over it and/or sticky labels added, the odds are that it is proving to be a very useful aid. In secondary schools, the test of how well IEPs are used is whether a teacher knows about a pupil's difficulties, plans accordingly and differentiates effectively in the classroom, science lab, studio, gym and so on.

The SENCO should seek feedback from pupils themselves and from supporting staff, but also be prepared to ask colleagues directly if the IEP is doing its job – and if not, asking how it can be improved. Performance management procedures in school should also address this issue, with subject leaders observing lessons and evaluating how IEPs – and behaviour plans – are being used.

Be realistic about what you expect class teachers to do. They have thirty pupils to think about, in a limited amount of time. Give them guidance about what is achievable in lessons, without spending hours on preparing individual task sheets. Many of these strategies may seem obvious to experienced SENCOs, but not to colleagues (and we do all need a little reminding from time to time), so include on an IEP some easy-to-do strategies such as those below.

- Explain new vocabulary – write it on the board, look at the spelling – get Sam to practise saying and writing new words, especially those with tricky spellings. (If he writes them in his homework diary, he can practise them at home with dad who has offered to help.) Display key words and topic vocabulary.
- Give instructions in bite-size portions; check Peter's understanding (the TA could do this).
- Use writing frames/recording formats (see stock in Room 12) to help Kim plan and complete written work.
- Allow Susie some thinking time for answering a question/preparation time before reading aloud.
- Make sure that Tom wears his glasses (and that they are clean), has his hearing aid switched on, has plenty of space to manoeuvre.
- Remember to face Kylie when you speak so that she can lip-read and see your facial expression.

Where an IEP *is* used, its design should allow for constant amending and updating. When pupils have significant learning difficulties, their targets will be described in small steps and it may be more appropriate for TAs working alongside the pupil to keep a (handwritten) 'running record' of aims and achievements in 'pupilspeak', as shown below.

Name:	Date:	TA:
What I tried to do …	What I did …	Next, I will …
Learn the difference between 'there' and 'their'	Used the correct word in 5 out of 10 sentences	Practise again tomorrow and try to get 10/10

These daily records can be clipped to the IEP to show the small steps taken to achieve a stated target (for example, 'to improve Spelling Age by 1yr, by the end of summer term', or 'stay on task for 10 mins'). See an example of an **Individual Behaviour Plan** on page 41.

Individual Behaviour Plan

photocopiable

Name: Year: Stage:	Start date: Review date: IBP no:	**Area of concern:** Disruptive behaviour **Strengths:** Good at sport, especially football **Teacher/Support:** TA Mrs Briggs provides general in-class support (mornings)
Targets: 1 To remain in seat during lessons. 2 To stay on task. 3 To avoid disrupting other pupils' work.	**Strategies for use in class:** 1 Seat at front, next to Jack or Ben. 2 Praise when on task. 3 TA to build in purposeful breaks during lesson; for example, get dictionary from bookshelf, give out worksheets. 4 Use record card to provide visual recognition of success (10 min slots). 5 Can opt to work in 'quiet corner'.	**Role of parent(s)/carer(s):** 1 To keep in touch with school and be informed of progess made. 2 To support work of school by providing treats as rewards when appropriate.
Success criteria: 1 No instances of 'off task' behaviour for a whole day. 2 Record card shows good level of on-task behaviour for week (over 50%). 3 No recorded instances of disruption for whole week.	**Resources:** 1 TA to supervise filling in of record card (to be signed by teacher). 2 Personalized record card. 3 Letter sent to parents at end of week. 4 Meet with mentor (Mr Lee, PE teacher) once a week.	**Agreed by:** SENCO: Parent/Carer: Pupil: Date:

WWW.CONTINUUMBOOKS.COM

SENCO AT A GLANCE
© LINDA EVANS (CONTINUUM 2007)

Helping Teachers to Identify Children with SEN and Plan Accordingly

Shifting responsibility for identifying pupils' needs to class/subject teachers means that they have ownership of the process and the ensuing provision. This is not to suggest that SENCOs should 'bow out' of assessing children – particularly the sort of diagnostic assessment that can pinpoint very specific areas of need and help to plan appropriate intervention programmes; but all teachers need to take responsibility for spotting pupils who need additional support. Observing pupils in lessons, looking at their work and posing questions to test their understanding will highlight difficulties. Many schools use a **Cause for Concern Sheet** for teachers to complete and pass on to the SENCO at regular points during the year (see example provided opposite). The names of pupils already on the SEN Intervention List (register) can be pre-entered to save time, with the opportunity for teachers to add new names as necessary. This sort of record can also be used to collect information for review meetings. You may need to remind colleagues to look out for those pupils who are 'quietly underachieving'; the noisy, badly behaved ones make themselves known, but others successfully hide their difficulties.

> You may need to remind colleagues to look out for those pupils who are 'quietly under-achieving'.

Setting appropriate learning objectives requires teachers to be sure about what a pupil knows and can do before setting targets for them. (This is particularly challenging in secondary schools, where subject teachers spend much less time with students and therefore take longer to become familiar with their strengths and weaknesses.) A lesson on mass, for example, might require pupils to weigh objects, compare weights, estimate the collective weight of several objects, add together actual weights in grams (and kilograms). But Melanie does not yet understand the concept of mass and confuses it with size (that is, 'big' must equal 'heavy'). The teacher's objective for this pupil must be to address her understanding of concepts of size and weight, before moving on to standard measures and complicated numerical operations.

Increasingly, teachers in mainstream schools are using P levels to help them set achievable targets for pupils with learning difficulties and report on small amounts of progress made. These describe performance which is pre-National Curriculum Level 1 and help teachers to differentiate for a wide spread of ability (www.qca.org.uk).

Effective differentiation is crucial to pupils achieving success and maintaining good self-esteem, and the SENCO can achieve a great deal by providing helpful INSET for colleagues. Too often, the lesson plan relies on TA support as the main means of differentiation, when in fact teachers should have a whole battery of differentiation strategies at their disposal. See examples of these on the sheet **Differentiation Strategies** (p. 44).

Cause for Concern Sheet

photocopiable

Class/subject group: **Teacher:**   **Date:**

Pupils on the SEN register are listed below, please indicate if they are making good progress. If you have concerns about them, please enter details. Pupils not previously identified can be added to the list, with details of difficulties encountered.

Pupil	School Action (SA) School Action plus (SA+) Statement (St)	Reading age/ NC level	Making progress (MP) or Cause for Concern (CC)	Details of difficulties observed

Differentation Strategies

photocopiable

You can differentiate by doing the following.

- Checking understanding of the lesson objective, expected outcomes, sequence of tasks

- Reviewing the readability of texts used in the classroom and employing strategies to support weak readers

- Making adaptations to equipment and/or providing special equipment (especially in science, D&T, PE)

- Using visual props and/or symbols to support understanding

- Providing writing frames to support recording

- Providing talking frames to support oral feedback

- Introducing alternative means of recording – for example, audio tapes, voice recognition software, diagrammatic/mind map recording, digital photographs of completed work, investigations in progress

- Using touch screens, switches and large-format keyboards

- Using software such as Clicker (Crick Software) to support writing

- Adapting tasks or providing alternative activities – breaking down new learning into small chunks

- Using a multisensory approach

- Providing and managing support from adults or peers

- Giving positive and helpful feedback throughout the lesson

- Allowing extra time for completion of tasks and/or providing opportunities for preparation time, perhaps with the help of a teaching assistant (remembering that children with special needs often have to make a lot more effort than other children to understand a new concept and complete a task)

NB: Technology offers excellent opportunities for differentiation of all kinds – from simply changing the on-screen font size and colour to using big-format keyboards and switches; from using spell checkers to installing networked software programmes to practice spelling. SENCOs can achieve huge changes in a short amount of time simply by introducing staff and pupils to appropriate technology. Contact one of the specialist companies for catalogues and advice on installation and training:

Inclusive Technology: www.inclusive.co.uk
Semerc: www.semerc.com
Widgit Software: www.widgit.com

Targeting and Planning In-class Support

Joint planning involving teachers and support teachers or TAs can result in the most effective differentiation. Support staff tend to know individual pupils very well and be able to anticipate prospective barriers to achievement. In the most successful partnerships, the TA is able to prepare the pupil for the work ahead, produce a suitable recording sheet or make sure there is appropriate software loaded on the laptop. This level of working takes time to develop, but a key role for the SENCO is making sure that TAs and support staff are deployed in the most effective way, and able to make a real contribution to pupils' learning and enjoyment. Lack of time is usually cited as the main obstacle to effective joint planning and evaluation – so you may have to devise a paper-based or electronic system of communication; involve the staff in deciding on what will work in practice, without being yet another chore. See the **TA Support Planning Sheet** (p. 46) as an example. This sheet could be pinned to a worksheet the teacher intends to use, or slipped inside the appropriate textbook for the TA to refer to and to ensure that the lesson is prepared for.

This is a key area for CPD in many schools. You can use the **Working Together** sheet (p. 47) to provide a basis for discussion and move staff forward in developing effective teacher/TA partnerships. TA support is always valued highly by teaching staff, and SENCOs often have to prioritize when there's not enough to go round (especially in secondary schools). Establishing the requirement for joint planning/evaluation can be one way of helping to allocate support where it will be most effective.

TA Support Planning Sheet   photocopiable

Teacher: TA: Lesson: Date:

Lesson Objectives:
Activities:

Type of support (pupils named where appropriate):

Support individual pupils in class	
Work with small groups of pupils in class	
Support whole class – with focus on …	
Teach individual/small group out of class	

Task	✔or ✘	Details
Help plan the lesson and suggest ways in which pupils with SEN can be supported		
Prepare materials for lesson: modify worksheets		
Distribute books/materials in class		
Support/teach alternative starter activity to small group		
Help teacher model/demonstrate skill to class		
Relay/interpret instructions		
Encourage listening and concentration skills		
Give subject-specific keywords and correct spellings		
Help write out work		
Provide notes to pupils		
Help pupils to organize thoughts and answers		
Encourage self-correction		
Question for understanding		
Help to maintain discipline (individual/class level)		
Correct written work/mark work during lesson		
Provide feedback on work to pupils		
Provide feedback to the teacher on pupil progress		
Assist with practical work		
Supervise work on the computer		
Encourage pupil participation in oral situations		
Encourage cooperation with others		
Encourage/help with correct recording of homework tasks		
Reward progress/effort		
Observe/assess identified pupils		
Tidy/clean up classroom after lesson		
Create displays in the classroom		

Working Together: Teacher and TA Partnership

photocopiable

Teacher: TA:

Lessons where support is provided:

Mon	Tues	Wed	Thurs	Fri

Please make time for an initial discussion to clarify roles and agree on ways of working. It may be useful to use the prompts below.

- ◆ How will you share lesson planning and other information?

- ◆ How will the TA be introduced to the class?

- ◆ What authority will the TA have in terms of behaviour management, sanctions and rewards?

- ◆ What will the TA be doing during a whole-class, teacher-led session; for example, starter and plenary? (For example, assessing pupils' responses; prompting; facilitating; recording.)

- ◆ What will be the main focus of support during lessons? (For example, identified students, small-group work on particular objectives.)

- ◆ Where will the TA work at different points in the lessons? Consider space available.

- ◆ Will you expect the TA to mark pupils' work?

- ◆ How and when will the TA give feedback? (For example, objectives achieved, behaviour observed, suitability of tasks/pace for individuals, any misconceptions.)

- ◆ What does the TA need to know for your lessons? (For example, curriculum information, health and safety issues, access to resources and planning.)

Helping Teachers to Monitor and Record Progress

As mentioned above, the P levels can be useful in recording small steps of progress and this is an area where TAs can provide valuable support to the teacher. Keeping a record of a pupil's achievements in a particular lesson can also contribute to the monitoring of progress. See the **Record of Support (1)** and **(2)** sheets on pages 49 to 50 and use these to record progress.

Monitoring for Inclusion

Lesson observations were mentioned in Chapter 1 as a way of monitoring the work of TAs, but in order to evaluate the level of inclusion across the school, class/subject teachers also have to be monitored. This will form part of the performance management reviews conducted by senior staff and a checklist is provided – **Monitoring for Inclusion** – to help in this and/or for teachers to use as a self-evaluation tool.

Record of Support (1)

photocopiable

TA:

Student:

Date	Lesson/teacher	On time?	Equipment?	Homework completed?	Quick to settle?	Followed verbal instructions?	Followed written instructions?	Concentration?	Participation?	Cooperation?	Able to work independently?	Understood lesson objective/outcome?	Tasks completed?	Progress towards IEP Target 1?	Progress towards IEP Target 2?	Progress towards IEP Target 3?	Comments: ♦ what worked well ♦ reasons for difficulties ♦ suggestions for future support ♦ strengths. (Continue on back if necessary but pass on more immediate information verbally to staff and/or SENCO.)

WWW.CONTINUUMBOOKS.COM

SENCO AT A GLANCE
© LINDA EVANS (CONTINUUM 2007)

Record of Support (2)

photocopiable

Pupil's Name: Class/group: Date:

TA/support teacher: Lesson:

Note:
- pupil's progress in terms of lesson objectives/IEP targets
- successful strategies for support
- next steps.

Monitoring for Inclusion

photocopiable

Class/subject teacher:	Support teacher/TA:	
Date:	Lesson:	Class:
Pupils on SEN register: SA	SA+	Statement
Details of lesson:		

Management and organization	Observed	Suggestions made
Well-organized room with distraction-free area available if needed		
Pupils grouped appropriately		
Evidence of positive attitudes to learning		
Clear objectives, shared with class		
Activities clearly explained/modelled		
Teacher checks pupils' understanding of tasks		
Time guide given		
Appropriate resources ready and reachable		
Behaviour expectations made clear		
Strategies in place for behaviour management		
TA knows what to do		
All pupils given opportunity to join in		
Teacher and TA communicate throughout lesson		
Teaching and learning		
Smooth transition between activities		
Activities suitably differentiated (input, outcome, resources)		
Multisensory learning experiences		
Effective support for pupils with additional needs		
New/required vocabulary displayed		
Visual timetable displayed		
Non-verbal support used (signs, symbols, pictures, text)		
Questioning used to good effect		
Pupils encouraged to work independently/ help each other as appropriate		
TA actively engaged in supporting as many pupils as possible		
All contributions recognized and positive behaviour rewarded		
Ongoing assessment used to guide/support pupils and give feedback		
Plenary used to check understanding and invite contributions from all learners		

3 Working With Other People: Professionals, Parents and Governors

Joint Working and Service-level Agreements

There will be pupils who need input from a range of services, and as SENCO you may well be the person who takes on the responsibility for pulling together the support from different agencies. These might include:

- education support services (behaviour support; counselling; educational welfare officer; student (learning) support service; sensory support service; educational psychologist)
- local Health Care Trust (medical specialist; dietician; physiotherapist, occupational therapist, speech and language therapist; psychotherapist)
- social services (for children at risk; looked-after children)
- police service (community safety officer; child abuse team; young offenders team)
- other schools or settings (special school or unit)
- voluntary/independent organizations.

The role of the key-worker is important in cases like this, pulling together assessments and paperwork to avoid repetition of information giving and to ensure that relevant information is shared (with the consent of the child/young person and parents/carers as appropriate). In the best scenarios, professionals are made aware of each other's work and are able collectively to provide an appropriate package of support. This relies on:

- identifying need
- sharing knowledge/information (with awareness of confidentiality issues)
- being clear about individual expertise and the role each professional is to play
- balancing resources with assessed need
- working towards the same goal
- understanding services, duties and limitations (including finances).

The key-worker – possibly the SENCO – acts as the point of reference for all concerned parties and liaises with the family. The key-worker will be responsible for arranging assessments and collating assessment information, organizing and running meetings and putting together a joint agency plan. Such a plan will:

- clearly set out the outcomes to be achieved for the child/young person (and possibly the family)
- define the accountabilities of everyone involved – who will do what, when and where (with costs)
- detail the processes of evaluation – how will we know if it's working?
- set out the arrangements for review.

Where different services are involved, a Service Level Agreement (SLA) may be drawn up. This is an agreement between users and providers of support services which specifies the service to be provided and the charge to be made. Many local authority (learning) support services already have SLAs in place, detailing what they offer in terms of pupil assesment/tuition, staff training, resources and opportunities to share good practice, with a sliding scale of costs.

In some cases, reciprocal agreements may be drawn up, where services between providers are exchanged rather than money changing hands. This can be particularly useful where a special school is providing outreach services for neighbouring schools and an example is provided – see **Service-level Agreement (Outreach)** on page 54.

In practice, joint working can be difficult; getting together three or four busy professionals from different agencies can prove a huge task – especially where funding is separate and different agencies have different priorities. These are not reasons to avoid joint working, but they are reasons to make sure that proper arrangements are in place and that everyone involved in a meeting or review comes away feeling that it was worthwhile and that they made a useful contribution. Make sure that accurate minutes are taken and agreed by everyone at the end of a meeting; this avoids disagreement later on, over who agreed to do what.

> Make sure everyone involved in a meeting or review comes away feeling that it was worthwhile.

Making arrangements for this type of working is very time-consuming indeed and, in a large school, the SENCO will almost certainly need someone to help by providing efficient administrative support. This person may help the SENCO or another SMT member by doing the following.

1. By setting up a comprehensive database of individuals from outside agencies, with:
    - a description of their role
    - details of when they work, which days, which hours
    - office base for working (may be more than one)
    - contact details – telephone (switchboard/reception, direct line, mobile, email).

Service-level Agreement (Outreach) photocopiable

Between **Wilton Lane Special School** (WL) and **Oak Tree School** (OT)

The purpose of this Agreement is to outline what each school will provide and how the recipients of services will support these activities.

WL will provide to OT:

1. A specialist teacher of children with ASD (Mrs Finton) to deliver training to all staff in the autumn term (2x twilight).
2. An HLTA to support two pupils in Y5 for two mornings each week (one term initially).
3. A telephone and email helpline to the SENCO and class teacher.
4. HLTA and Mrs Finton to attend review meetings as appropriate.

WL will expect OT to:

- Make arrangements for the twilight INSET sessions, with PowerPoint projector set up and all staff attending.
- Ensure joint planning/evaluation time for the HLTA and Mrs Finton and SENCO/Class teacher.
- Give plenty of notice of review meetings to be held, times, venue, agenda and so on.

OT will provide to WL:

1. Science coordinator Mr Timms to provide staff INSET (2x twilight).
2. Mr Timms to teach Y5 groups for Science for two mornings each week (one term initially).
3. Mr Timms to provide materials/equipment and support class teachers in lesson planning for Science (email helpline + 'surgery' on Tuesday lunchtime).

OT will expect WL to:

- Make arrangements for the twilight INSET sessions, with PowerPoint projector set up and all staff attending.
- Take care of all equipment/resources on loan and return to OT after use.
- Inform OT of any changes to Y5 timetable.

The Agreement will be subject to review at a meeting between all concerned parties on 4 Dec 2007.

Signed: Date:

Headteacher Wilton Lane Special School

Signed: Date:

Headteacher Oak Tree School

Keeping this information up to date can be a significant job in itself. One way of doing this is to print out the information for each person and get them to confirm or change details on a regular basis when they come in to school (see example on page 55).

Name: Sheila Williams	**Please check information and initial/date to confirm that it is correct, or change appropriately.**
Post/responsibilities Occupational therapist (children 0–11yrs)	SW 07.10.09
Office address: **Newcross Health Centre** **Fleming Road**	SW 07.10.09
Contacts: Office tel. **0121 XXX YY** Mobile XXXXXXX Email: SW@nhstwest.uk	SW 07.10.09
Times available: **Tues, Wed in term time 8.30–4.30** (usually best to telephone between 8.30 and 9.30 am)	SW Our office has moved to Lord St. Please note the new tel. no: 01299 xxx xxx

2 By contacting individuals with as much notice as possible to arrange meetings or assessment/therapy sessions for children. And by confirming the arrangements in writing or by email.

3 By booking/preparing an appropriate room and informing individuals where this is, including staff on reception. For meetings, by making the room as inviting and comfortable as possible: having a table to sit at is better for making notes and gives a more business like impression. By arranging for refreshments and explaining where cloakrooms are. If there is a shortage of space in school, by considering asking a nearby school/college or Community/Health Centre for the loan of a room.

4 By sending out any relevant information prior to the meeting so that people can come prepared – including an agenda and any specific requests: 'Sheila – please come prepared to give us an update on Ben's progress and your opinion about his ability to start joining in with PE lessons.'

Planning and Chairing Meetings

Being able to chair a meeting efficiently is a very useful skill – and one worth developing as it will save you time, and win the respect of participants.

1. Prepare properly for the meeting – make sure you know what you hope to achieve. Try to avoid coming out of the meeting with a load of extra work – think beforehand about what can be shared between participants, and how much can be done during the meeting itself – for example can an admin assistant take minutes? (On a laptop?). Be sure to document what different people have agreed to do – and by when. This is particularly important when senior decision-makers are involved and have to commit to funding a child's provision. If that person moves on, is ill or on holiday, and there is nothing 'official' recorded, the whole business of getting things sorted out can be delayed. A template for recording meetings, **Record of Meeting**, is shown opposite.

2. During the meeting, make sure that everyone speaks and makes a contribution (check beforehand whether it's appropriate for someone to send in a written report rather than have to attend the meeting). Guard against one person 'hogging the floor'.

3. Be assertive in keeping everyone 'on task' and keeping to time. Avoid acronyms and jargon – make sure that there is a shared understanding of terms; confusion about what exactly is meant is one of the biggest barriers to successful joint working. (Arranging for joint training can do a lot to alleviate this sort of problem.)

4. At the end of the meeting, recap main points and decisions taken. Agree a date and time for the next meeting if necessary. Finish on time – this shows that you value people's attendance and will improve your chances of getting them back next time.

> *Avoid acronyms and jargon – make sure that there is a shared understanding of terms.*

SENCOs may be involved in multidisciplinary meetings about children in care. A Personal Education Plan (PEP) must be drawn up for each child, forming part of the wider care planning. Different PEP formats are used by different local authorities, but all will:

- set clear objectives for the child, relating to academic achievement and personal and behavioural targets, both in and out of school
- identify who will be responsible for carrying out the actions agreed in the plan, with timescales for action and review
- cover the child's achievement record (academic and otherwise)
- identify development needs and set short- and long-term targets.

The SENCO (or the designated teacher) should be involved in agreeing and reviewing a PEP along with the child (according to understanding and ability), the child's parent and/or relevant family member or carer, and the social worker. If a looked-after child joins the school without a PEP, the designated teacher should pursue the matter with the child's social worker who is responsible for initiating it. A child's PEP is particularly useful at times of transition, whether from primary to secondary school or from one setting to another. It enables information to move quickly with the child, so that they can be placed appropriately and provided with the support and services they need.

Record of Meeting

photocopiable

Purpose of meeting:

Date: People present:

To be discussed:	Main points/comments	Agreed action (what, who, when)
1		
2		
3		
4		
5		

Date for review:

Signed:

Parents

The *Code of Practice, Removing Barriers to Achievement* and *Every Child Matters* – all recent legislation and guidance – highlights the importance of working in partnership with parents. For children with SEN in particular, it's important to have shared aims about enabling them to achieve their potential and to have consistency of approach in supporting them through difficulties. Parents have a critical part to play in their children's education and hold key information that can help you to identify difficulties and find ways of helping. They may have a totally different perspective on what the 'problems' are and may well have worked out strategies to use in the home that can be usefully adapted to work at school.

All SENCOs know, however, that it can be challenging to get parents 'onside'. It's useful to remind ourselves of a few things from their point of view, for example

> 'I have five other children to worry about.'
> 'I work long hours and don't have time for …'
> 'I can never get to speak to school staff when I need to.'
> 'Meetings are always at the wrong time for me.'
> 'They don't realize that I have to catch two buses to get there.'
> 'I never liked school and I'm not surprised that my son doesn't either.'

Establishing a good relationship with parents may not always be easy but it's an important part of the SENCO role to do everything possible to get them onside.

- Find out about a child's home circumstances – will the key figure at home be a mum, dad, grandparent, older sibling or foster carer? Make sure that you have the correct name (and title) of the key person/s to use in letters, emails and telephone calls.
- At the first meeting, introduce yourself and explain your role in school – avoid any jargon or acronyms.
- Listen to the parent/carer at least as much as you expect them to listen to you. They know their child better than anyone.
- Be professional but friendly, stick to the 'agenda' and steer the parent/carer back on course when necessary (we all love talking abut our kids and minutes can easily turn into hours!).
- Be positive, but honest and realistic, about achievements/strengths, targets and areas for development.
- Provide accessible and clear guidance about how parents/carers can support their children. Many schools provide a booklet for parents of children with SEN, explaining the different ways of supporting them in school and how parents and other family members can help.
- Keep open a line of communication – for positive feedback as well as problem sharing (home–school diary, weekly phone call/email, half-termly meeting). This is especially important as children get older and the informal chat with parents as they drop them off at/collect them from school no longer happens.
- Adopt an 'open door' policy for parents, or where this is impractical, try offering a 'phone surgery', advertised in the school newsletter and on the website.

> **PARENT PHONE SURGERY**
> Oak Tree School runs a phone surgery for parents who wish to discuss their child's learning needs with the SENCO. The surgery runs from 4.30pm until 6.00pm every Wednesday in term time.

Any sort of meetings in school can be anxiety inducing for parents. They can feel intimidated by the school building, the officiousness of admin staff, the 'superiority' of teaching staff and senior managers. They may have had less-than-positive experiences themselves at school and still be carrying around some negative feelings. There are several ways of reassuring them.

> *Parents may have had less-than-positive experiences themselves at school and still be carrying around some negative feelings.*

- Make a home visit – meeting parents on their own territory can make a big difference and there will then be a 'friendly face' to give them moral support at parents evening or reviews. The visit may be made by the SENCO or another member of staff, an LSA/TA or another parent. Take an interpreter/signer along if this will help to put parents at ease.
- Use a comfortable area for meetings in school – family/community room, staffroom, library – preferably with adult-size chairs and a cup of tea. Make them feel welcome and valued. Respect confidentiality and ensure that conversations are private. Encourage parents to make a few notes to bring with them to a review meeting, or give them a questionnaire/checklist to complete – see **Parent/Carer Questionnaire** (p. 60) for an example. This will enable them to be better prepared and feel more confident. Be aware of the difficulties some parents/carers face in fitting in with 'school hours' (shift work, child care, transport); be flexible where possible and offer an early/late meeting time.
- If you want family members to actively support a pupil at home, be prepared to offer some clear guidance on how to do this. It's easy to assume that if we say or write 'share a book every night', or 'help Sam with spellings', that people know exactly what we mean – often they don't. Providing notes can help, or running a parents workshop to explain and demonstrate approaches to reading, writing, numeracy or behaviour. Providing opportunities for parents/carers and children to work together can also be very effective.

The Parent Partnership Service provides a range of support for parents including: a telephone helpline; parent supporters to help with paperwork and support parents at meetings; written information about different kinds of SEN; interpreters and signers; a directory of local support groups; and independent mediation between parents, local authority and school. It may be helpful to put parents/carers in touch with their local branch; details are available from the national website (www.parentpartnership.org.uk).

Contact a Family (CAF) is the UK-wide charity providing advice, information and support to the parents of all disabled children – no matter what their health condition. The charity also enables parents to get in contact with other families, on both a local and a national basis and provides information on a wide range of disabilities and medical conditions (www.cafamily.org.uk).

Parent/Carer Questionnaire

photocopiable

Name of parent/carer: Name of child:

Is your child happy to come to school? Does s/he have friends?

Is your child making good progress? What does s/he like best about school?

Are teachers supportive? Are there any particular lessons s/he finds difficult?

Is there anything about school that your child worries about?

Are there any problems at home?

Is there anything else you would like to discuss with us?

Pupil Participation

Involving pupils in decisions about their IEPs and types of support provided is something that everyone acknowledges as a 'good thing' but, in practice, is not always well done. Put yourself in their shoes; would you be happy with the level of input you were afforded? It may not always be appropriate for a child to attend review meetings, but a one-to-one with the SENCO or TA/mentor beforehand can provide useful information about 'client satisfaction' and an insight into how a child is responding to the support on offer.

Involving children and young people in shaping their education is essential to effective inclusion. All pupils, including those with SEN, should:

- evaluate their own learning (at a basic level, thumbs up/down or smiley/sad face; at a higher level, highlighting one good thing about their learning, one element that could be improved)
- think about how they learn best and what/who can help them
- set personal targets and plan how to achieve them
- understand how progress against targets can be measured.

Many schools now have designated times for pupil review meetings, where class/form teachers or year tutors discuss progress and any issues with pupils. The pupil questionnaire: **How am I Doing at School?** (p. 62) could be used for such a review; or given to the pupil to complete (possibly with the help of TA, parent or mentor) prior to such a review or a joint working team/statement review. The language may have to be adjusted to ensure a pupil's understanding (or converted to sign/symbol language). Where a pupil has individual support from a TA, it may be useful for someone else to help out with the review; this may reveal, for example, whether there are issues about the TA–pupil relationship.

Another aspect of pupil participation is class/school councils, and you may need to remind staff that these should have input from pupils with SEN and disabilities.

How am I Doing at School?

photocopiable

Name: Date:

What I like most about school is …

Some things I do really well at school are …

Something about school that I worry about or find difficult is …

People who help me at school are …
They help me by …

Something that would help me to enjoy and do better at school is …

Something I would change about school if I could is …

Record of achievement, success and merit awards, certificates, etc *(including after-school clubs, teams, etc)*

Two targets: by _____ (date) I will:

1

2

I will know I have been successful when_____

Governors

Every school should have a 'designated' governor for SEN and/or Inclusion who takes a special interest in the SENCO's work and ensures that everyone on the governing body has an awareness and understanding of SEN issues. Governors have important statutory duties in relation to pupils with SEN and should ensure that:

- appropriate provision is made for any pupil with SEN, as set out in the CoP
- all staff who teach a child with SEN are informed about that pupil's needs
- effective identification and assessment procedures are in place
- the LA and other schools and services are involved in provision where necessary
- pupils with SEN are included in the life of the school
- disabled pupils are not subject to discrimination in respect of admissions, the quality of education they receive or exclusions
- the school makes 'reasonable adjustments' to meet the needs of a disabled pupil
- there is an annual report to parents on SEN provision
- parents are notified about any SEN provision made for their child
- funding for SEN is used appropriately
- SEN provision is continually monitored and impacts on the SDP.

In order to fulfil these duties, the designated governor will need to have a copy of the SEN Policy and Development plan and regular contact with the SENCO and members of the support team.

In one school, the designated governor visits on every first Monday of the month and has lunch with a group of pupils and the SENCO in the dining hall before spending half an hour in the lunchtime study club. The SENCO then updates the governor over a cup of coffee in her office, with the help of a short report on new developments, evaluation data, changes of staff, training delivered/attended and so on. See the template provided for your **Report to Governors on SEN/Inclusion** (p. 64). Once a term, the governor extends his visit to observe a lesson during the afternoon and attend the support team meeting after school. This means that the governor is very 'in touch' with what is going on in terms of SEN provision, the staff involved and (importantly) the pupils, and can confidently update fellow governors at every meeting. The SENCO and governor have an excellent working relationship and can rely on one another for mutual support.

This is of course, an ideal scenario; in many cases, the governor has a full-time job which prevents them from making this type of commitment. But many employers are sympathetic to this sort of voluntary work and it's always worth asking about the possibility of a couple of hours 'time out' each month to make this sort of visit.

Training for governors is offered by many local authorities, often in the evenings, and offers an opportunity for governor and SENCO to attend together; it can provide a more palatable way of learning about SEN legislation, guidance and good practice than ploughing through reams of printed information.

However you achieve it, time spent in updating the governor/s on SEN issues is always worthwhile and fulfils an important aspect of the SENCO role.

Report to Governors on SEN/Inclusion photocopiable

Date:

1 Numbers of pupils on SEN register

School action	School action +	Statement

Comment:

2 Changes to intervention programmes:

Comment:

3 CPD delivered/attended:

Comment:

4 Monitoring activities:

Comment:

5 Joint working activities:

Comment:

6 Review meetings:

Comment:

In Conclusion

You will have many more ideas about how to audit, evaluate and improve what you do as a SENCO – especially if you are conscientious about your own professional development and keep up to date with what others are doing. Perhaps the most important thing to remember is that you don't have to do everything all at once. The scale of the role can be daunting – but take one or two areas at a time and get them right before moving on. With the current pace of change in education, the chances are that even the best provision will need to change in some way, before too long. Try to determine what is good, what is developing and what needs to be developed – then plan how to improve and move forward as best you can.

The SENCO role attracts the most caring people among educational professionals, and the most conscientious; it can be easy to see the glass as half-full and dwell on what still needs to be done. Make sure that you acknowledge everything that you, your colleagues and pupils have achieved each day/week and remember to celebrate your successes – no matter how small.

Glossary *photocopiable*

ADD	Attention Deficit Disorder
ADHD	Attention Deficit Hyperactivity Disorder
AEN	Additional Educational Needs
ASD	Autistic Spectrum Disorder (Autism)
BESD	Behavioural, Emotional and Social Difficulties
BP	Behaviour Plan
CA	Chronological Age
CoP	Code of Practice
CP	Cerebral Palsy
CPD	Continuing Professional Development
DfES	Department for Educational Skills
DCSF	Department for Children, Schools and Families
EAL	English as an Additional Language
ECM	Every Child Matters
EP	Educational Psychologist
GEP	Group Education Plan
HI	Hearing Impairment
HLTA	Higher Level Teaching Assistant
IBP	Individual Behaviour Plan
ICT	Information and Communications Technology
IEP	Individual Education Plan
INSET	In-service training
ITT	Initial Teacher Training
LA	Local Authority
LEA	Local Education Authority
LS	Learning Support
LSA	Learning Support Assistant
MLD	Moderate Learning Difficulties
NC	National Curriculum
NFER	National Foundation for Educational Research
NQT	Newly Qualified Teacher
OT	Occupational Therapist
PDR	Professional Development Review
PEP	Personal Education Plan
P scale/P levels	Set of optional indicators for recording the achievements of pupils with Special Educational Needs
RA	Reading Age
RB	Reading Buddy
SA	School Action
SA(SpA)	Spelling Age
SA+	School Action Plus
SDP	School Development Plan
SEF	Self-evaluation Form
SEN	Special Educational Needs
SENCO	Special Educational Needs Coordinator
SLA	Service Level Agreement
SLT	Speech and Language Therapist (SALT)
SMT	Senior Management (Leadership) Team
TA	Teaching Assistant
VAK	Visual–Auditory–Kinaesthetic
VI	Vision Impairment
VR	Verbal Reasoning

Bibliography

Booth, T. and Ainscow, M. (2002) *Index for Inclusion*. Bristol: Centre for Studies on Inclusive Education.

Cheminais, R. (2004) *How to Create the Inclusive Classroom*. London: David Fulton Publishers.

DfES (2004) *Removing Barriers to Achievement: The Government's strategy for SEN*. (see www.everychildmatters.gov.uk/socialcare/disabledchildren)

East, V. and Evans, L. (2006) *At a Glance: A Practical Guide to Children's Special Needs*. 2nd edn. London: Continuum.

George, J. and Hunt, M. (2003) *Appointing and Managing Learning Support Assistants*. London: David Fulton Publishers.

Gross, J. and White, A. (2003) *Special Educational Needs and School Improvement*. London: David Fulton Publishers.

Hayward, A. (2006) *Making Inclusion Happen*. London: Paul Chapman Publishing.

House of Commons (2006) *Special Educational Needs, Volume 1: The Report of the House of Commons Education and Skills Select Committee*. July, ref HC478-1.

McNamara, S. and Moreton, G. (1997) *Understanding Differentiation*. London: David Fulton Publishers.

Peterson, L. (2006) 'SENCO Noticeboard', *Special!* (NASEN), autumn.

QCA (2002) *Including All Learners*. London: Qualifications and Curriculum Authority.

Spooner, Wendy (2006) *The SEN Handbook for Trainee Teachers, NQTs and Assistants*. London: David Fulton Publishers.

TDA *The National Standards for Special Educational Needs Co-ordinators*. The Training and Development Agency website, April 2006, www.tda.gov.uk.

Useful Websites

www.bda.co.uk	BDA British Dyslexia Association
www.cafamily.org.uk	Contact a Family (CAF)
www.cricksoft.com	Crick software (Clicker and so on)
www.dfes.gov.uk	DfES/DCSF
www.downs-syndrome.org.uk	Downs Syndrome Association
www.everychildmatters.org.uk	Every Child Matters
www.inclusive.co.uk	Inclusive technology
www.nasen.org.uk	NASEN (National Association for Special Educational Needs)
www.oaasis.co.uk	OAASIS Office for Advice, Assistance, Support and Information on Special Needs
www.ofsted.gov.uk	Ofsted
www.optimuspub.co.uk	SENCO update
www.parentpartnership.org.uk	Parent Partnership Service
www.qca.org.uk	QCA (Qualifications and Curriculum Authority)
www.semerc.com	Semerc
www.teachingtimes.com	Special Children
www.widgit.com	Widgit software